CASE STUDIES IN

CULTURAL ANTHROPOLOGY

GENERAL EDITORS
George and Louise Spindler
STANFORD UNIVERSITY

———————

CHANGING JAPAN

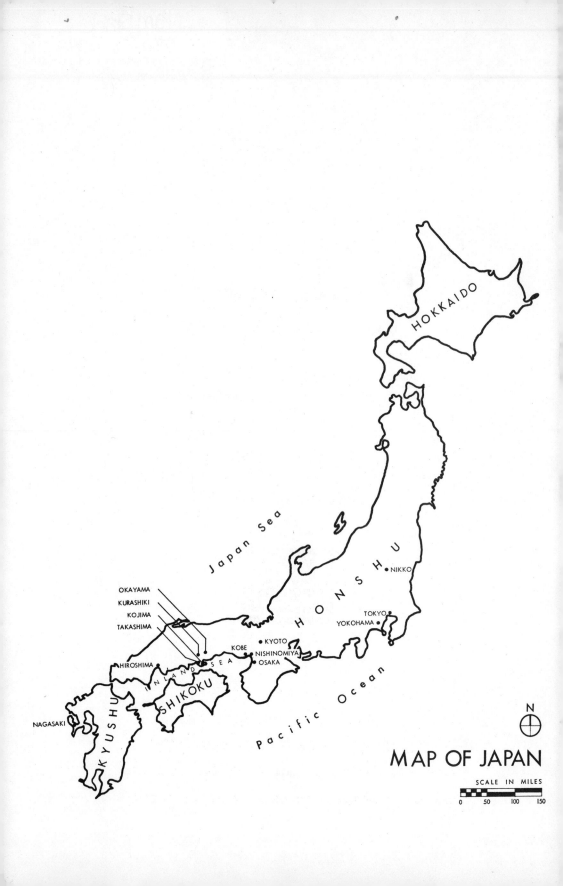

OKAYAMA
KURASHIKI
KOJIMA
TAKASHIMA

HIROSHIMA

NAGASAKI

Japan Sea

HOKKAIDO

H O N S H U

•NIKKO

TOKYO
YOKOHAMA •

•KYOTO
KOBE
NISHINOMIYA
OSAKA

I N L A N D   S E A

K Y U S H U

SHIKOKU

Pacific Ocean

N

MAP OF JAPAN

SCALE IN MILES

0   50   100   150

CHANGING JAPAN

Second Edition

By

EDWARD NORBECK

Rice University

HOLT, RINEHART AND WINSTON

NEW YORK   CHICAGO   SAN FRANCISCO   ATLANTA

DALLAS   MONTREAL   TORONTO   LONDON   SYDNEY

Library of Congress Cataloging in Publication Data

Norbeck, Edward, 1915–
  Changing Japan.

  (Case studies in cultural anthropology)
  Bibliography: p. 107
  1.   Japan—Social life and customs—1945–
I.   Title.
DS822.5.N67   1976   309.1′52′04   76-2709
ISBN: 0–03–017546–1

Foreword

About the Series

These case studies in cultural anthropology are designed to bring to students, in beginning and intermediate courses in the social sciences, insights into the richness and complexity of human life as it is lived in different ways and in different places. They are written by men and women who have lived in the societies they write about, and who are professionally trained as observers and interpreters of human behavior. The authors are also teachers, and in writing their books they have kept the students who will read them foremost in their minds. It is our belief that when an understanding of ways of life very different from one's own is gained, abstractions and generalizations about social structure, cultural values, subsistence techniques, and the other universal categories of human social behavior become meaningful.

About the Author

Edward Norbeck was born in Canada and received his training in oriental culture and anthropology at the University of Michigan. He has taught at the University of Utah and the University of California, Berkeley, and is presently Professor of Anthropology at Rice University. His interest in Japanese culture goes back to his years of residence in Hawaii before World War II, when he first came into contact with many people of Japanese descent. During the war he served in the military intelligence in matters connected with Japan. He is the author of the books *Takashima, A Japanese Fishing Community*, 1954; *Pineapple Town—Hawaii*, 1959; *Religion in Primitive Society*, 1961; *Religion and Society in Modern Japan*, 1970; *Religion in Human Life*, 1974; co-editor of *Prehistoric Man in the New World*, 1964; *The Study of Personality*, 1968; *The Study of Japan in the Behavioral Sciences*, 1970; *The Anthropological Study of Human Play*, 1974, and *Ideas of Culture*, 1976, and has written many scholarly articles and essays concerning Japanese culture and various other anthropological subjects.

About the Book

As Dr. Norbeck points out, internal contrasts within Japanese society have always been sharp, and they have grown rather than diminished as time has passed. There are many ways of life in Japan, and in their variety they reflect

v

the unevenness of change in a dynamic society that has moved from feudalism since 1868 to industrial urbanization, and that has recovered since 1945 from a crushing military defeat to attain now its greatest period of prosperity.

One way for the anthropologist to cope with this kind of heterogeneity is to focus on a manageable segment of the whole society—usually a small community. Where cultural heterogeneity and rapid change are both significant forces this approach has its limitations, if the purpose is to gain perspective on the contrasts apparent in the larger framework of society. Dr. Norbeck has solved this problem brilliantly. In this relatively brief case study he puts both change and variety in sharp focus. First he provides a summary introduction that sets the broad limits within which inquiry may proceed, and then penetrates directly to the central process of change in Japanese society by contrasting life in a modern rural community to life in Osaka. These contrasts are given a special poignancy by describing two very different families: one an extended family household in rural Takashima; the other a small, status-achieving urban family whose male head is the second son of the village family. Though the contrasts between village and city are indeed sharp, the reader can anticipate the urban condition even as he reads about life in the Matsui family of Takashima, for rural life has not remained static and there are differences in the beliefs and attitudes of the generations in the extended family household that reflect the general secularization and urbanization of Japanese life.

About the Second Edition

After a return trip to Japan ending in December 1974, Edward Norbeck wrote a new preface, a new conclusion to Part 1, "The Modernization of Japan—A Decade Later," and a new Part 4, "The Urbanized Rural Community," all included in this new edition of *Changing Japan*. Little is needed in this foreword to introduce the new edition, for the author's preface has done this well. What is most striking to us, the editors, who have worked in urbanizing small communities in Germany and are interested observers of the Spanish scene, is that many universal processes which override cultural differences appear to be set in motion by modernization and urbanization.* The standard of living rises, self-sufficiency declines, congestion and environmental pollution increase, the countryside tends to become depopulated while the metropolitan areas expand more and more; farming becomes a part-time occupation except for a few large commercial enterprises; the family shrinks in size but the population as a whole continues to increase; older people increasingly live apart from their children and a problem of what to do with the aged has arisen; rituals and religiosity decline even though religious movements do occur; voluntary asso-

* See G. L. Spindler, *Burgbach: Urbanization and Identity in a German Village*; R. Barrett, *Benabarre: The Modernization of a Spanish Village*; J. Friedl, *Kippel: A Changing Village in the Alps*; J. M. Halpern and B. K. Halpern, *A Serbian Village in Historical Perspective*; Z. Salzman and V. Scheufler, *Komárov: A Czech Farming Village*, all in the Case Studies in Cultural Anthropology series.

ciations increase in number and in functions; women seek new rights; the esthetic quality of life declines; and everything costs more. Some of these changes appear to be linear; others seem to fluoresce and recede. Many may be considered symptomatic of more fundamental processes that we have no very good way of describing as yet. And despite the overriding character of modernization, each culture appears to retain certain qualities that distinguish it from other cultures, despite massive and probably universal changes.

This case study is particularly impressive because the people of Takashima are still a part of a distinctive community that has survived despite a great change in the physical environment and loss of the means of subsistence possible within it. A part of that change made industrial employment possible for most able-bodied wage earners. And it is good to know that although the level of environmental pollution exceeds anything known in the United States, all of the principals of the families and the personal vignettes of the first edition are still alive. The pollution itself is still bad, but the worst appears to be over and serious continuing efforts are being made to contain it, though the long-term effects upon the local inhabitants or the world biosphere are not known.

Particularly striking is the fact that, as in Germany and Spain, despite what appear to be the inhuman and even degrading effects of industrialization, modernization, and urbanization (the last is the term least well understood), the people choose the conditions of the present over those of the seemingly more esthetic and humane past. Perhaps there is nothing more inhuman and degrading than poverty and hunger. It is to Edward Norbeck's credit that he has been able to see the changes from the peoples' point of view and that he has not allowed a romanticized idealization of the recent past as he observed and appreciated it to interfere with an objective description of the present.

GEORGE AND LOUISE SPINDLER
General Editors

January 1976

Preface to Second Edition

Ten years have passed since the original edition of this book was published, a decade in which the conditions of human life have changed almost everywhere. Some of the changes that have occurred in Japan are well known to the rest of the world. Ever more, Japan has become a successful international competitor in manufacture and trade and an international power. Correspondingly, its citizens are today richer and have higher standards of living than formerly. Clear evidence of this affluence lies before the eyes of much of the world in the persons of the many Japanese nationals who now travel to foreign countries as pleasure-seeking tourists. Many other changes have taken place within Japan, of course, but these are generally little known to the outside world except to a few scholars and a still smaller number of diplomats. These changes are in matters of daily life, the family and other social units, and a host of ideals, values, attitudes, and customs.

In one way or another the changes of the past decade are all continuations of trends already well established ten or more years ago, and they thus represent no radical departures from past conditions. Japan today continues to be recognizably Japan, a nation in which the old exists along with the new in ways that are distinctively Japanese.

Now and then the original edition of this book is outmoded in its particulars, but the themes and trends to which the particulars refer continue to hold. Only a few statements of fact concerning national conditions that appear in the original edition are today wholly inaccurate. One inaccuracy has already been implied; for most people, unremitting thrift is not necessary today to allow mere survival. Another inaccurate statement concerns privately owned automobiles; today many rather than a few people own cars. The use of oxen in agriculture, uncommon even ten years ago, appears to have come to an end. An additional statement that needs correction concerns the publishing of books; for reasons that are unclear, the number of books currently published in Japan, although large, no longer exceeds that published in the United States.

A few statements appearing in the original edition will likely soon be quite inaccurate. The nation's colleges and universities have expanded so that they now fairly well accommodate the many young people who seek admission to them, and suicide among students who fail to pass college entrance exams, long principally a subject of talk rather than a common occurrence, has become statistically rare.

These emendations complete the list of statements requiring correction. Changes that represent development of established trends cannot be disposed of so simply. Since the trends described in the original edition continue to exist today in more highly developed form, what is needed to provide an up-to-date view of Japan is principally an account of additions. Accordingly, the contents of the original edition are here reprinted except for a brief passage at the conclusion of Part 1 which describes principally the author's field research in Japan. Rewritten to bring it up to date, this passage appears at the end of this preface. Revisions in the new edition consist of additions describing changes of the past decade, which are presented under two headings.

One addition, appearing at the end of Part 1, is an overall account of national developments entitled "The Modernization of Japan—A Decade Later." The second addition concerns a phenomenon that attained its highest incidence and speed in recent years, the urbanization of rural communities. Part 4, entitled "The Urbanized Rural Community," describes an actual community which changed from rural to urban industrial life in a period of only a few years beginning in the late 1960s. The community described is the hamlet of Takashima in central Japan, the scene of the events described in the original edition, and reprinted here, as Part 2, "A Rural Family." A rural community a decade ago, Takashima is today incorporated in a thriving industrial city and the lives of its residents are daily more and more those of suburban industrial workers. Industrial employment is by far the most common occupation in Japan, of course, and the lives of the people of Takashima today are thus fairly representative of the conditions of existence of the residents of an uncounted but great number of additional communities of the nation. The narrative accounts of the two families, urban and rural, that appear in the original edition are brought up to date in the concluding pages of Part 4.

Field research upon which the original and revised editions of this book are based was conducted by the author in 1950–1951, 1958–1959, 1964–1965, 1966, and 1974, principally in Okayama prefecture of southwestern Japan, Miyagi prefecture of northeastern Japan, and the metropolitan areas of Tokyo and Osaka. Short trips elsewhere have taken the author to most parts of Japan. Throughout, emphasis in field research has been given to changes in Japanese society and culture and to factors that have brought about the changes. The community of Takashima was investigated intensively in 1950–1951 and 1974 and visited briefly in 1959 and 1964.

E. N.

January 1976

Acknowledgments

For their aid in the preparation of this book, I wish to express my sincere thanks to Richard K. Beardsley, Hiroshi Mannari, Kiyomi Morioka, Rachel and David C. Stubbs, Norihisa Suzuki, my wife, and many unnamed Japanese citizens who have patiently and courteously answered my many questions. I am indebted to the National Science Foundation for a grant-in-aid that made my research during 1964–1965 possible.

In the preparation of the revised edition, I am thankful to Akira Ōyama, Shiro Moriwake, Takaaki Sanada, Masako Hayashi, and, once again, to Hiroshi Mannari. I am also indebted to many people of the community of Takashima, especially Minoru Matsui, and to informants in the neighboring community of Shionasu. I am grateful to the National Science Foundation for a grant-in-aid supporting my research in Japan for six months ending in late December 1974.

Contents

Left: Country grandparents in their finest formal clothing. Right: New Year's date in Osaka.

Right: Street scene before the shopping center in Kōri danchi, a public housing project in the Osaka area.

Below: Street scene in a rural community, Okayama Prefecture.

Harbor and terraced farm-lands, Takashima.

Right: Street scene in Osaka.

Below: The buraku of Takashima, "High Island," partial view.

Japanese Society and Culture

Introduction

JAPAN is a land of jet airplanes, modern medicine, giant industrial concerns, the most elaborate and efficient network of railroads known to the world, a nation committed to scientific progress and international trade. It is a nation of readers that publishes more books annually than the United States. To its population the scientist is a familiar figure who makes outstanding contributions to international knowledge in physics, medicine, nutrition, agronomy, and other fields of scientific research. Its literacy rate is one of the highest in the world, and its colleges and universities cannot accommodate the young men and women who clamor for admission.

Japan is a nation of mass communication, second only to the United States in the number of television sets owned by its citizens. It is a land where business executives receive annual incomes as great as a million dollars, and where luxury products at fabulous prices—jewels, furs, gowns by famous European couturiers, imported automobiles, and anything else the world produces—are abundantly available. It is a land of European classical music and progressive jazz; of bars, cabarets, coffee houses, theaters; of baseball, skiing, and golf; of endless streams of dating young couples. The streets of its cities throb with industrial activity by day and at nightfall become wild jungles of neon lights crowded with pleasure seekers. It is a nation devoted to the pursuit of happiness and one that holds democracy as an ideal. It is a nation where life is secular, where most of the citizenry disclaims faith in any religion.

Japan is a land where oxen plough rice paddies side by side with miniature tractors; men and women plant and transplant rice by hand; the average citizen owns no car, has never ridden in an airplane, lives in an intensely cramped house or apartment, and practices the utmost thrift in order to survive. It is a land of *kubuki* drama, *sumo* wrestling, the tea ceremony, and—for the wealthy or those with large expense accounts who are so inclined—of the traditional song, dance, and personal ministrations of *geisha*. The modern youth of Japan who fails to pass entrance examinations to a university, and others who feel their honor has been impugned, may resort to tradition and wipe out their shame by suicide.

Japan is a land where religion is ever evident, where one is seldom out of sight of Buddhist temples or Shinto shrines whose festivals attract enormous crowds of onlookers. It is a land that inters its dead with traditional Buddhist rites. It is a land of occult supernaturalism, where emotions and wishes triumph over reason in affairs that touch close to the heart. To seek health and good fortune its citizens utter mystic formulae and purchase from religious establishments amulets of almost infinite variety. To foresee the future its citizens look to divination. The streets of its cities are sprinkled at night with specialists in fortune telling, and residents of Tokyo make use of a battery of brilliant red pay telephones in the heart of the city to learn their horoscopes for the day. To protect themselves its citizens are careful to see that marriages, journeys to distant places, business ventures, and other matters of importance are conducted at times that are auspicious according to ancient lore transmitted from China. Yama-bushi, the mountaineer priests who came into existence nearly a thousand years ago, perform incantations to exorcise evil spirits and illness. Carpenters refuse to build houses without performing traditional rites to appease and win the favor of supernatural beings.

Japan is a land of shopkeepers, of tiny industrial enterprises, of poverty and suffering, of arranged marriages, and of the most serious dedication to work, duty, and obligation. It is a land of social hierarchy, where the voice of superiors carries great weight, and where the wants of the individual must stand in second place to those of the group.

These words are meant to express the familiar saying that Japan is a land of contrasts. Many of these have long existed in Japanese culture, and others have come with modernization. It is especially important to note that the contrasts have grown rather than diminished as the years have passed. Any description of Japanese culture that seeks to be general and also accurate must proceed with qualifications. There are many ways of life in Japan, ways that differ in large part because they reflect unevenly the changes that have come about within the past several decades. The statistically typical Japanese culture does not conform with reality as known to any group of Japanese people.

In 1868 Japan saw the end of over two centuries of self-imposed isolation from the rest of the world. Japan of the time may be described as a small and culturally backward country, a nation of impoverished, illiterate peasants under the control of a small group of hereditary rulers and their retainers. The process of catching up culturally with the Western world began at once and proceeded at a dizzying pace that suffered only brief interruption during the years that Japan prepared for and waged World War II. Since the end of the war, the process of cultural change has been accelerated. The world has marveled at the speed with which the nation recovered economically from the ravages of the war. Japan now enjoys the most favorable economic conditions of its entire modern history, and the trend is toward increased prosperity.

These statements imply that many social changes have also occurred. Japan is in fact in a state of cultural flux that might be called peaceful boiling. There is, of course, continuity, but what describes today does not accurately describe tomorrow.

It is inappropriate to describe the way of life of a modern rural community as typifying the Japanese nation. It is also improper to describe as typical the manners of life that are fully urban. Part of the urban population of Japan is only a half step removed from the country, and the vast majority of the population of Japan's cities stem from rural backgrounds within the last two or three generations. Through their grandparents a substantial number of Japanese citizens living today had direct contact in their childhoods with the feudal culture of the Tokugawa era (1603-1868).

With the aim of presenting in a few pages an account as representative as possible of the whole nation, I have chosen to bridge rural and urban life by taking as my subject a family whose members include both city and country dwellers, and thus quickly becomes more than one family. Such families are indeed representative. In 1868 approximately 85 percent of the nation was engaged directly in agricultural employment. By the end of World War II this figure had shrunk to less than 50 percent. It has declined in recent years at an annual rate of about 2 percent to a present figure well below 30 percent. The foregoing statistics represent principal employment rather than full-time employment, and therefore present a deceptive picture of the nature of the labor force actually engaged in agriculture. Many of the farmers are women who are also housewives and mothers; many of the male farmers are part-time workers in industry or in other nonagricultural occupations.

It is both impossible and inappropriate to give more than a partial account of changing Japanese culture in a case study depicting the life of a small number of people. A short account such as this must also omit much that is important in Japanese culture and useful in gaining an understanding of ways of life. For these reasons it is useful first to discuss certain aspects of Japanese culture that cannot otherwise be dealt with explicitly.

Pre-Modern Social Structure and Values

At the end of the Tokugawa era, approximately a century ago, Japanese society was divided into hereditary classes. Social and political organization was rigidly hierarchical, and many mechanisms served to maintain sharp borders among the social classes. At the top were less than three thousand members of the nobility and their near-noble retainers, the *samurai*. With their families the *samurai* numbered about two million persons. Below them stood the masses, about thirty million commoners, most of whom were farmers or in other rural occupations as fishermen and foresters. Below the commoners stood another class of perhaps several hundred thousand persons, the Eta, who lived in separate communities and formed an outcast group denied many of the privileges of commoners. Scattered about the nation and sometimes locally concentrated were various much smaller groups of people associated with specific handicrafts and other humble occupations who were semioutcasts, not so deeply dyed with baseness as the Eta. Although legally commoners rather than outcasts, these peoples were regarded and treated by the general population in much the same way as the Eta. Perhaps the largest of these groups was composed of communities of boat-dwelling fisherfolk, migrants who followed fixed annual routes of travel chiefly in the Inland Sea and the waters off Nagasaki.

As elsewhere in the world, the fundamental unit of social life was the family, but it had characteristics of organization unique to Japan. It was through the solidarity of kin and community that life was made possible, and ties of kinship were intimate. In ideal if not always in practical reality, the individual had no existence apart from his identity as a family and community member. Populations were customarily tallied by numbers of households rather than individuals, and the desires and needs of the group were paramount.

Relatives beyond those living in face-to-face contact in a single dwelling were also important. Variably large and important kin units composed of households related through patrilineal lines existed in many parts of Japan. These kin groups, called *dōzoku* and a variety of other local names, consisted of a founding household (*honke*), the richest and most powerful of the group, and a variable number of branch households (*bunke*). As circumstances allowed or required, branch households were established by the main household, which gave lands and dwellings to junior sons who, under the rule of primogeniture, were not provided for. A third generation of offshoots of branch households might also be included. The *dōzoku* was hierarchical, with the main household at the apex, and was held together by a set of values and sanctions of compelling force. The fundamental tie was economic but, in characteristic human fashion, it was rationalized as a bond of honor and emotion. Privileges and obligations extended mutually between superiors and inferiors. Although the greatest giving was upward, those who stood in inferior positions were made to feel privileged by benefits conferred from above, and those in superior positions were compelled by honor to fulfill obligations to those below them, for whose welfare they were responsible. When property was great and kin were few, unrelated households were sometimes incorporated into the *dōzoku* by rites that made them into quasi or fictive kin whose relationships with the head household were much like those of normal kinship.

Most of the nation lived in small rural communities, largely self-sufficient, that were sometimes composed entirely of kin and almost always included many kinsmen. A rural community might consist of a single *dōzoku;* more commonly it held two or three of these organizations of kin and fictive kin. Where, as in much of southwestern Japan, the *dōzoku* had not developed strongly or had already disappeared, kinship nevertheless held great importance and its ties went far beyond the confines of the nuclear family of husband, wife, and children. Like the family, the small community was tightly united. For the ordinary person life was confined almost entirely to association with family and community members.

As with the nation as a whole, the small world of the ordinary citizen was one of hierarchy. Within the family the male head stood supreme, and males stood far above females. Primogeniture generally prevailed, and the eldest son held a position of prestige. Daughters married out, and they and their descendants became identified with the genealogies of their husbands. Younger sons were unnecessary to the continuity of family lines and often constituted a social problem. They were provided for in a variety of ways, all less desirable than the treatment accorded the eldest. If their families had sufficient wealth, they might be set up as heads of branch families. Often they were adopted by households lacking sons. Adoption might take place in infancy or when a boy had reached young adulthood, at whatever age was locally regarded as suitable for marriage. The young man then married the daughter of a family lacking a son, assumed the surname of her family, and became its legally adopted son and heir. Whether adopted or natural, the eldest son and heir was morally bound to provide for his parents after they became old. Once he became head of the household, he also provided in appropriate fashion for such younger siblings as might not yet have reached maturity.

Where the normal channels of kinship did not serve, for lack of personnel or for whatever other reason, recourse was sometimes made to fictive kinship resembling that sometimes found in the *dōzoku*. Individuals, and sometimes whole households, performed rites that bound them to other individuals or households as "relatives" with mutual privileges and obligations much like those of conventional kinship. Here, too, hierarchy prevailed. Characteristically, one individual stood in the position of "parent" (*oyabun*), and the other was his "child" (*kobun*). Although one parent might have several or many "children," who became as brothers and sisters to one another, fictive kinship among people close to each other in age and modeled after the relationships of brothers and sisters had little development. Where it did exist, the relationship was based principally upon emotional rather than economic ties.

When whole families entered fictive kin relationships of this kind, the positions of superiority and inferiority were less clearly defined than in the *dōzoku*. The relationship was also less strongly economic than that of the *dōzoku* and looser in affective bonds, and it applied to two families rather than to a united skein of households.

Kinship terminology was commonly used among the persons united by ties of fictive kinship. Commonly also, kin terms were employed for all people of the small community, related or unrelated, as long as they were not members of households markedly different in social status. The familial nature of Japanese society of the time is strongly evident in these practices of personal address. Relatives of whatever degree of relationship, remote or near, and unrelated members of peer families were characteristically addressed by one of a range of names denoting close kin. Although many terms of reference existed for more remote genetic relatives and in-laws, these were not employed in direct address. Dependent upon their relative age, all members of the small community who were older than the speaker were ordinarily addressed as grandfather, grandmother, aunt, uncle, elder brother, or elder sister. Those younger than the speaker were called by their given names. "Grandfather," "grandmother," and other names denoting superior age were marks of respect and honor; one liked to be called by these names. "Grandfather" and "grandmother" were also general terms meaning old man and old woman that one might use in either reference or address for total strangers. The importance of status in kinship relations is also clearly revealed by usages of kin terms that often applied among *dōzoku* groups and fictive kin. Members of a branch family of a *dōzoku* might address members of their founding family who were in fact younger than the speaker by names indicating superior age. Thus a young girl of a founding family might be called "elder sister" by the middle-aged head of a branch of her family. When fictive kinship applied among individuals, the senior was commonly called "father" or other names derived from that term, and he called his fictive sons by their given names in the manner of ordinary kinship. When two or more persons were "children" of the same fictive parents, they customarily stood toward each other as "elder brother" and "younger brother" or "elder sister" and "younger sister," and used the terms of address ordinarily appropriate for these relationships. Relative age was not the only consideration involved; a young man with a forceful personality or one who for other reason stood in a position of authority among a number of fictive brothers might be addressed as "elder brother" by those older than he.

Hierarchy and kinship were not the only organizing principles of society. Along with them and important to the maintenance of life, although less striking to the eye, was a network of social groups along horizontal lines. Wherever kinship and fictive kinship were inadequate for the task, communal and cooperative groups of various kinds arose. Called *kō*, *kumi*, *kumiai*, and other regional names, these were cooperative organizations concerned primarily with farming, fishing, and community tasks that required the joint efforts of many people. Some concerned affairs of the small community, such as maintenance of roads and other communal facilities and property. Others were religious associations that provided aid to bereaved community members and performed other religious tasks when deaths occurred. Various important associations centering on work connected with agriculture and fishing, such as the building and maintenance of irrigation systems, were anciently established. In communities where the *dōzoku* organization of kin and fictive kin was powerful, these relatively democratic associations had little development except when they concerned religious affairs or other matters that did not threaten the authority of founding households. Throughout the nation the common-interest association was nevertheless common. It was well developed in areas where farmland was in the hands of small owner-operators rather than under the control of landlords with extensive holdings operated for them by tenant farmers.

The unit of membership in the common-interest associations was ordinarily the family rather than the individual, even when membership was based on considerations of sex, age, and friendship. In theory, and largely in actuality, these associations were egalitarian. Their internal organization, to be sure, was in part hierarchical, and the voices of the socially most eminent members carried the greatest weight. Any formalized association with functions affecting the whole community did in fact, however, represent the community in its membership. Whether households were composed of few or many people, each had one representative, ordinarily the household head, and each household ideally had equal voice in decisions.

The religious life of the people followed the tenets and practices of both the native Shinto religion and Buddhism, which reached Japan by way of China in the sixth century. In addition, the people followed many supernatural beliefs and practices of diverse origin that were not a part of either Shinto or Buddhism. These included forms of divination, taboos, faith healing, and many other magical practices. As the centuries passed, Shinto and Buddhism had come to resemble each other in many ways and adherence to both created no conflict for the people. Moreover, the two religions had become functionally compartmented with relation to many important aspects of life. Where they overlapped, procedures were much alike and both were characteristically followed. The villager was a parishioner of the Shinto shrine of the local tutelary god and a parishioner of a temple of one of the Buddhist sects.

Shinto was the religion of daily life. In addition to local tutelary gods, a host of other supernatural beings who could favor or disfavor man needed respect, honor, offerings, and prayer. One of the important ways of maintaining the favor of the gods was to remain ritually clean by avoiding, or following special procedures to remove, harmful pollution arising from contact with death and blood. Buddhism was preeminently the religion of death and ancestors; funerals and numerous commemorative services were the primary Buddhist ceremonies of the home. Great annual festivals, Shinto and Buddhist, were scattered through the year in close accord with the agricultural seasons. Other ceremonies marked important events, such as the construction of dwellings and boats, and birth, maturity, and other crises in the lives of individuals.

Among the people religion was eminently practical, concerned with the problems of life. Priestly theology was a matter of little interest or concern. Religion for the ordinary man was action, not philosophy. It told him something of the nature of the universe, what to do to avoid misfortune, how to escape from misfortune when it struck, and how to gain assurance that life would proceed in normal and desirable ways. Religion was also a primary form of entertainment. The ceremonial calendar was elaborate and included several great festivals which were occasions for feasts, rest, pleasurable association with visiting relatives and other community members, and the enjoyment of religious pageantry. At Obon, the great Buddhist festival of midsummer, festivities included community dancing in which people of all ages participated. This was a time when some of the ordinary rules were suspended, and young men and women of the country might then with tacit approval seek lovers. Pilgrimages to distant shrines were religious acts that held high value. Conferring supernatural benefit, they were also times of pleasure when one could forget his daily worries and obligations for days and even weeks or months at a time.

Above all else, the activities of daily life and the religion concerned the work which provided a livelihood. Crops had to be planted, cared for, and harvested; forest lands tended; and the sea tilled for its harvest of fish. Bonds of kinship and of communal membership were the means by which these tasks were accomplished and they were also the means of meeting human emotional wants. Life was intensely personalized.' Economic transactions were not merely commercial exchanges; they were also explicitly social and affective events. The behavior of any individual was intimately the concern of many others.

Sharply defined procedures of social intercourse for all conceivable occasions were one of the most outstanding features of life. The long isolation of Japan from the rest of the world coupled with relatively static conditions of culture provided ideal circumstances for the rigid formation of social classes. Part and parcel of this social rigidity was the formation of minutely defined rules of behavior for every recognized class and category of human beings. Rules governing behavior between categories that stood in superior-inferior positions to each other were especially elaborate and important. Formal prescriptions told *samurai*-commoner and husband-wife how to conduct their relations and the precise nature of their mutual obligations and privileges. Greater privilege was expectably held by superiors. A man could divorce his wife with ease; a woman could divorce her husband only with great difficulty. Wherever property or the related continuity of familial lines was of any importance, formal prescriptions instructed how and whom to marry, and were effective in preserving social boundaries. Insignia of status in forms of speech, gestures, dress, ornaments, and other personal possessions were abundant and jealously guarded.

The ethical person of a century ago was one who understood his role thoroughly and did not pass its boundaries. He knew his place and all the rules that defined it. There were, of course, laws, rules, and understandings concerning moral offenses such as theft, incest, and murder. But these were of a different nature, applying in essentially the same way to all. Infraction of these rules did not so much reflect upon one's social status as upon his status as a proper human being, and these rules were generally so thoroughly ingrained that they did not require or receive the kind of reinforcement given to the conventions governing interclass behavior. Rules of ethical behavior that were explicitly and repeatedly taught a century ago were, in short, largely what the Western world would call etiquette—conventions that applied to relations between different classes of human beings.

Rules of interclass privilege, obligation, and social intercourse were formally taught in schools as codes of ethics to *samurai* and noblemen, who, by vying among themselves for social advancement within their classes, were the most serious threat to preservation of the social scheme. Certain Confucian principles of ethics were well suited to the Japanese social conditions of the time and these, in secular rather than religious guise, formed the core of the formal teachings. Loyalty to superiors, filial piety, and *rei*—a term, often translated into English as "etiquette," that implies an ethical code of interclass and interpersonal behavior—were prime virtues.

These values also diffused to the common man, who received less formal but ample instruction concerning his place in society. A *samurai* had the privilege of beheading a commoner who failed to obey the rules of etiquette, but few heads seemed to have rolled on this account. The dominant sanction for ethical behavior did not lie in acts of this kind, but in the numerous penalties and rewards implied by the terms "face" and "loss of face." Society was rigidly pigeonholed. Each virtuous member knew his place and the places of others and guarded them. The opinion of others was then a potent force toward propriety. Moreover, the individual was always identified as a member of a group, so that unethical behavior on his part reflected upon the group—the family, the community, or the *samurai* as a class. Legal sanctions of various kinds expectably reflected, and reinforced, the social order. Important among these were sumptuary laws that defined many of the visible insignia of status, and extended to such things as types of clothing and hairdress. Religion, although touching upon the realm of morality only lightly, served to reinforce the social order through Shinto beliefs in tutelary gods, the divine origin of the emperor, the ancestor worship of Buddhism, and in other ways.

The Modernization of Japan

The customs sketched for Japan a century ago have by no means disappeared without a trace. The long span of the Tokugawa era allowed a very firm set. The Meiji era (1868–1912) that followed saw many and great changes, but these occurred in ways that allowed, even encouraged, the continuation of a social order and supporting values that in many ways did not radically differ from the past. Ruth Benedict's discussion (*The Chrysanthemum and the Sword*) of Japanese values presumably existing during World War II is highly suggestive of the late nineteenth century, perhaps in part because her interpretation centers on ideals that were already old-fashioned if not obsolete. The century since the beginning of Meiji has, in short, seen both cultural change and continuity. Changes occurring during any short segment of the century may be regarded as quantitative, but in the long view they are undeniably qualitative. Japanese society of today is far from that of a century ago. But let us look at the changes of the century more specifically.

A century ago Japan was a nation composed principally of peasants whose way of life conformed in general outlines with that of folk societies elsewhere in the world. The fundamental stimuli leading to and guiding the changes that occurred subsequently have been economic. After Japan emerged from its isolation, industrialization began at once. The process of its industrialization has been described in many historical accounts that are readily available, and we shall here note only that it proceeded extremely quickly and peacefully. A trend of movement began at once from rural occupations to industrial and urban callings. These occupations in turn depended for their existence not only upon technological knowledge imported from the West but also upon the more fundamental sciences from which the technology was derived. In the space of a few decades Japan enthusiastically inspected, and sometimes embraced, all that the West had to offer in the sciences and arts as well as in technology.

Many centuries earlier Japan had similarly welcomed Chinese culture, which brought to Japan a flood of innovations. The mode of reception of Chinese and the later Western culture was the same, one of selective adaptation rather than wholesale borrowing, adaptation that permitted innovations to become assimilated without suddenly obliterating the old ways and causing violent social upheaval. Foreign culture that conflicted seriously with established ways was rejected. The Confucian idea that an inadequate ruler should be deposed, for example, was anathema to the Japanese, to whom the continuity of family lines in fixed positions of status was a value of prime importance. When individual members of any social group were incompetent, means other than frank disbarment were preferred, means that preserved social forms and individual and group honor. Throughout, the acceptance of Western as well as Chinese culture resulted in assimilations that had a distinctively Japanese cast.

In 1941, at the time Japan entered into war with the United States and Europe, profound changes had taken place peacefully in almost all sectors of life. No other nation of the modern world had undergone such drastic and self-sought cultural changes under conditions of internal peace in an equally short period of time. Japan was an international power with a population of seventy millions, heavily industrialized, a nation learned in science and technology if not yet an innovator in these fields. It was a nation of literate people, under the control of military rulers who maintained their power and waged war by forcefully imposing upon the population ideals and values that changed social conditions had already rendered partially obsolete. The recognition of personal ability was vital to the existence of the nation, but individualism was strongly discouraged. The strict guarding of hierarchical place in society—whether achieved by individual efforts or ascribed—was a lesson taught over and over again via the press, radio, and other media of communication, and in the schools. Filial piety, loyalty to superiors, and loyalty to the nation as embodied by the emperor were the keynotes of the time. *

The *samurai* were long gone. With the exception of the imperial family, such of the nobility as remained had not been supported by the society since the end of the Tokugawa era. As members of the nobility they did not hold political control. Yet political control of the nation was still in the hands of an autocratic few. Many women were wage earners and, by virtue of their economic status, had in fact gone far toward breaching the gap in social standing between themselves and male members of society. Yet women were told of their inferiority and lacked legal equality. The nuclear family, composed of husband, wife, and their children, had long since become the prevailing form of the urban family, and ties to relatives in the country and deceased ancestors had thinned. Yet filial piety and reverence for ancestors were ideals forcefully expounded. The nation was committed to science; and yet the military rulers exhorted the nation to worship an emperor of divine origin. *

The crushing defeat that Japan suffered in World War II may be seen in some respects as a boon rather than a calamity. Changes forcibly brought about by the military occupation loosened many shackles. It is not surprising that social values and ideals consciously taught in Japan should have been outdated. Although change was remarkably swift, at no time was it revolutionary. The industrialization of Japan had proceeded along its own lines, lines that made use of the existing social order. Rationales, the concepts that man devises at best half-consciously to make his way of life seem worthwhile and proper, expectably lag behind the cultural circumstances that lead to their formation. A society under the tight control of military leaders retaining outmoded views of the nature of their society could be all the more tardy in articulating a realistic and compatible rationale. Contrary opinion could be expressed only at the risk of life and property.

Considerable support for the foregoing statements is provided by the events of the military occupation. The seemingly drastic changes enforced by the occupation authorities were perhaps not so drastic. When the occupation ended, no successful movement toward reversion to earlier social conditions occurred. These circumstances do not appear to depict a compliant society that yields to any form of authority. Instead, the changes wrought by the occupation seem to be a continuation, a speeding up, of trends already well under way. Important among the innovations brought about by the occupation were a land reform, which freed tenant farmers from the heavy thumbs of landlords; extension of the voting franchise to women; the abolishment of primogeniture; and a revised constitution that gave much increased freedom to the individual, including freedom of religion. None of these was out of keeping with the social scene. Even land reforms were not new; Japan had had several lesser reforms of its own, the last of which was conducted during World War II.

Other postwar innovations, some instigated by occupation authorities and others by the Japanese themselves, are abundant, and many of them are too well known to need recounting here. Within ten years after its resounding defeat in the war, Japan was firmly back on its feet economically and showed increased agility. Industrialization proceeded at a quickened pace, and Japan came to depend more and more for its livelihood upon international trade. Intimately connected with industrialization were several developments in agriculture. The land reform brought quick returns in economic prosperity for farmers and the whole nation. Improved techniques and mechanization of agriculture and the incentive to exert added effort that came from individual ownership of farms greatly boosted agricultural yields, particularly in the impoverished backwoods or northeastern Japan. These changes also freed farm labor, which in turn found much improved opportunities for employment in the cities. By 1960 Japanese agriculture faced a crisis that arose in part from the very changes that had spurred its development. Rising prices of commodities and services necessary to the farmer made it difficult for him to wrest a living from the small farm plots that the law allowed him to own. The small size of individual holdings at the same time strongly inhibited the development of large-scale mechanization and mass production. The customary response of the rural male has been to seek additional part-time employment and, increasingly, to take full-time employment in industrial plants in nearby cities. By 1960 the shortage of farm labor was acute and the Japanese citizenry had come to speak of the feminization of the nation's agriculture. With rueful humor, farming came to be called "san-chan nōgyō," agriculture practiced by the three chan (an intimate term of address), grandfather-chan, grandmother-chan, and mother-chan. These problems of labor and efficient farm management will doubtless be met in the future by another land reform authorizing larger holdings and thus permitting intensive mechanization that reduces needs for manpower.

Other noteworthy developments included a great expansion of national programs of social welfare. Laws enacted since World War II that directly or indirectly affect the population have dealt with public health, family assistance, and insurance for unemployment, accident, sickness, death, old age, and loss of crops and livestock. National health insurance is socialized medicine, and it brings the cost of modern medical care down to levels that the ordinary citizen can afford. Although meager in many fields as compared with social welfare programs of England or the United States, these nationalized forms of social benefit represent great changes over prewar times and they expand year by year.

Along with increasingly successful industry has come increased specialization in labor, rising incomes, rising standards of living, and higher levels of education. Japan is very much a part of the world, and, since its welfare depends so heavily upon international trade, it is vitally interested in world affairs. None of the technical innovations of Europe and the United States is unknown to the citizens of Japan. Fashions in food, clothing, music, literature, sports, and entertainment tend to be international, and Japan is now in these and other realms of culture sometimes the innovator rather than merely the emulator. But some of the old Japan remains. These words may well be said of nearly every aspect of life. A casual glance at one of the great industrial cities of modern Japan reveals much that is common to cities elsewhere. Hotels, restaurants, clothing, taxis, streets, traffic signals, office buildings, shops, theaters, feminine hair styles and cosmetics are much alike. If one attempts to weigh similarities against differences, the things that Japan holds in common with the rest of the industrialized nations of the world are perhaps greater in number than those that differ. If one seeks differences, he may also find them, some obvious and others difficult for foreign eyes to see.

As one proceeds from the urban giant Tokyo to the smaller cities and to the country towns, the similarities decrease, but even the most isolated mountain or island community is in touch with the rest of the nation and shares its changing culture. The modern farmer is not a peasant, but is better regarded as a specialist among other specialists. Rural communities are an integral part of the industrial nation, a part far from self-sufficient that is charged with raising animal and vegetable foods. The modern farmer is seldom even officially a resident of a village. A continuing process, begun in the late nineteenth century, of amalgamating the thousands of formerly independent small communities into towns and cities has left only a small number of politically independent villages. Thoroughly developed mass media of communication and a great network of public trains and buses keep all parts of the nation in touch with each other.

And what has happened since the end of the Tokugawa era to the family and other kin groups, the common-interest associations, the structure of Japanese society in general? Some of the major trends may be summarized as a decline in the size and functional importance of the family and other kin groups, a weakening of the bonds of kinlike personal ties with unrelated persons, a change in patterns of authority within the family and elsewhere, and the emergence or increased growth of many impersonal institutions that provide economic and social security. Social classes have taken form following occupational lines, and all indications point to the growth of a huge urban middle class.

The nuclear family is the prevailing form throughout the nation. At least until the young go out into the world as adults, however, ties between familial members remain intimate. When relatives beyond husband, wife, and their children live under one roof and form part of the familial unit, these are customarily the aged parents of the household head and the family is rural rather than urban. In the city a sentiment has grown against living with one's parents, parents-in-law, or mature children, and the idea is not a total stranger to rural residents. Father's voice has lost a good deal of authority and mother's has gained. Younger sons are often at no disadvantage as compared with the eldest son, and sisters and new brides have lost some of their meekness. To prepare them for an adult life that is likely to take them away from farming, younger sons and even daughters of rural families may receive more formal education than eldest sons, who are ordinarily expected to remain on the farm. The mother-in-law who attempts to dominate her son's bride is in danger of being branded as "feudal," a demeaning word. A common postwar saying is that two things have grown in strength since the war, stockings—now of tough nylon—and women.

The relationship between man and wife is both more nearly equal and more intimate than in former times. This trend of change is part of a group of alterations in familial relations, some of which represent complementary emphases and de-emphases. As other social devices have taken over various of the former roles of kinship, the familial continuity through the generations is both less important and more difficult to maintain. The status of the eldest son thus holds less eminence, and its loss of importance has been accompanied by a rise in the position of wife and mother. At the same time, the strict supervision of marriage has become less important. Conventions of former times discouraged intense bonds between men and women, for these endangered the position of preeminence of the eldest son. Relations of intimacy and quality between man and wife endangered familial continuity by detracting from the father-son relationship and by placing authority in the hands of women. The new bride was ideally the lowest member of the household. In her youth a woman was traditionally under the domination of her husband and in her old age under the authority of her eldest son. In their roles as bearers and rearers of children, women were necessary mechanical appurtenances to a scheme of social structure which had provisions for continuity that involved many people and which was made to seem far more important than the relations between any two individuals. Proper men did not admit to romantic love for their wives; instead they spoke of them and to them as lowly creatures. Many other customs insured that women did not endanger the operations of the social machine.

Under the conditions of Tokugawa times, a low social position for females was congruous, and romantic love could find no approval either as a mode of selecting mates or as a desirable relationship between man and wife. It was only among people of lowest social classes, those lacking property and confined to egalitarian association with others of bottommost station, that men and women ordinarily married for love. Modern conditions of life provide increasing encouragement to romantic love and to lifelong attachments between spouses. The wife who walks some distance behind her husband on streets and roads has become a curiosity.

One of the many additional indications of the diminished importance of kinship is provided by present customs of using kin terms. Today they find less frequent use, especially for distant relatives and unrelated persons, and the use of personal names has grown. Kin terms long ago ceased to be appellations of respect and honor.* The modern woman is often none too anxious to be called "aunt" or "grandmother," and it is of course possible deliberately to insult by choice of a kin term suggesting that the addressee has lost the premium of youth. In this matter, too, it seems reasonable to think that the changed culture of Japan offers an explanation. Where romantic love between husband and wife finds encouragement, a desire on the part of men and, especially, of women to appear attractively young seems congruous. The modern Japanese wife gives growing attention to her personal appearance, and the commercial beauty industry of Japan has become a vast network of establishments providing cosmetics and services that reaches down to the smallest community.

The *dōzoku* has nearly disappeared. Some semblance of its old form is said still to be preserved among a few families of great wealth that control industrial and commercial concerns, and reports of its continued existence come now and then from a few rural areas. In most of rural Japan where the *dōzoku* was strong at the end of World War II, the land reform gave it a death blow. In many rural communities there is still talk about main households and branch households, as handy points of reference in tracing genealogies, but the formal ties and obligations are gone.

Fictive kinship has had an interesting career. In the earlier stages of the industrialization of Japan, the *oyabun-kobun* flourished as a social device transitional between the peasant and the industrial society. Young men and women migrating to cities entered this relationship with their employers or supervisors, and labor was often recruited on this basis. Today the *oyabun-kobun* relationship in its old form is common only at the fringes of society, in the world of professional criminals and prostitutes, where the economic innovations connected with legal employment have not penetrated. In the world of law-abiding citizens, the formal *oyabun-kobun* has generally been transmuted into milder forms of paternalism and these permeate Japanese society.*

As compared with circumstances in the United States, Japanese society continues to give much importance to kinship and to personalized ties with unrelated people. Industrial and commercial concerns are heavily paternalistic, looking into and after the welfare of their personnel in ways that go far beyond the demand of coldly rational business.* Small family enterprises remain very common and even the smallest shops and business concerns may provide living quarters for unrelated employees, especially the young and unmarried. Thus the firms take on many of the aspects of family enterprises. Large industrial firms frequently maintain apartments for married employees as well as dormitories for single people, and also often provide recreational facilities for their personnel. Labor unions are most frequently company unions. Nepotism in practices of employment is standard and often thoroughly approved. In the religious world priestly posts are customarily inherited. University professors are often still masters, and the students who become associated with them are their disciples. Leaders of gangs of criminals are also masters, who look after the welfare of their followers. No segment of Japanese society may be described as entirely free of familism, but even here continued trends of change are evident. The "progressive" inveigh publicly against paternalism, and the primary qualification for important positions in the worlds of industry and finance is personal ability. Commercial concerns have grown larger, rendering personalized relations more and more difficult to maintain, and the growth of the large business enterprises has been accompanied by the bankruptcy of many small concerns, which form the greatest strongholds of familism. The emphasis in employment shifts increasingly toward the recognition of talent and toward impersonality in employer-employee relations.

The functional substitutes for kinship that have emerged—institutions of social welfare, banks, labor unions, schools, courts of law, common-interest associations, and many other social and economic devices—continue to grow in importance. Among these, common-interest associations loom importantly in both city and country, and certain of them have assumed positions of vital importance to the rural resident. Any farming community of the nation includes among its residents members of twenty-five or more associations concerned with economic matters, community affairs, religion, and recreation. Of these, the agricultural cooperatives, in their postwar form, are the most important. These are the agency through which the farmer obtains machinery, tools, fertilizer, education in new techniques of agronomy, loans of money for farm improvement, insurance on crops and livestock, and much else. The cooperative is the farmer's bank for savings accounts as well as loans, the normal agency for sale of crops, and its social activities may provide much of the recreation available to the rural family. Under the circumstances of modern urban life—for the country as well as the city has become urbanized—common-interest associations offer a number of advantages. Their growth in Japan, as elsewhere, has marked a transition from strong reliance upon kinship and personal ties. Associations are highly elastic; kin groups are not. Associations may be formed, changed, or dissolved to meet altered circumstances, and their presence or absence does not disrupt family or community membership in any consequential way.

Various of the modern associations of Japan are modeled after American counterparts and bear English or English-derived names. The Parent-Teachers' Association (Pee-chee-eh) and 4-H (Yon-eichi) are examples introduced during the military occupation after World War II. Fraternal organizations stemming from the West that have high prestige in Japanese cities are the Rotary International and the Lions Club. Many other associations that have goals of social reform or humanitarian aims also resemble organizations of the Western world, especially of the United States, and have doubtless often been inspired by the foreign organizations. But here caution must be used. Common-interest associations are ancient in Japan as well as in the West, and they are a world-wide feature of human society, when circumstances encourage or allow their formation. When governmental control during the preceding century allowed the people of Japan to do so, they showed no reluctance to form their own common-interest associations, many of which had aims of social reform. Associations that appear to be entirely Japanese have sprung up thickly since the end of World War II, and their growth should not be interpreted as a mere copying of foreign social features. As an indication of the rising position of women, it is noteworthy that one of these is a large national organization called the Housewives' League (Shufuren) that seeks with considerable success to improve conditions of daily life and to combat social evils.

For the modern rural resident three kinds of social affiliation are highly important: membership in the immediate family, composed of those who live under a single roof; membership in common-interest associations; and membership in the community. Social solidarity in the face-to-face living community of the country remains strong, even when the little community is administratively part of a town or city. Since rural associations connected with agriculture and fishing are extremely important forms of self-help that depend upon communal cooperation, their growth to outstanding prominence since World War II has probably contributed to the solidarity of the small community. At the same time, however, these associations are linked nationally with others, and thus they also help bring the rural resident into the nation.

For the modern urban family, community membership is less important an issue, but familial life is intimate. Urban common-interest associations abound, but their importance is watered down by the easy availability of impersonal institutions of credit and finance and by matters of geographical residence. For the urban dwellers there are also greater opportunities to satisfy affective needs through informal groupings of friends, commercial places of entertainment, and formal or informal associations composed of fellow employees.

The movement from country to city, toward increased industrialization and increased depersonalization of life continues. As the nation's population approaches one hundred million, Tokyo and the other great industrial cities are congested beyond belief. Rapidly expanding systems of public transportation between and within cities cannot meet the mounting demands. Public transport companies in Tokyo and Osaka must hire employees whose task it is to push passengers into train and subway cars so that the doors may close. Demand for intercity transportation is so heavy that the sale of tickets must be handled in special ways to avoid scalping and other abuses. The traveler may buy a ticket three weeks before the date of travel, at which time a fixed, small part of the tickets are sold, usually within a few hours. One week before the day of travel the large remainder of tickets is offered for sale. During the several seasons of greatest travel, queues form at stations to wait overnight for the opening of the ticket offices the following morning. To accommodate those queueing for tickets and waiting for trains, during 1964 the Japan National Railways twice erected in the plaza before its Osaka station a giant circus tent said to shelter 10,000 persons. The number of intercity trains has long been vast, and it was augmented in 1964 by super-expresses traveling at speeds up to 130 miles per hour on a new track be-

tween Osaka and Tokyo, the area of heaviest traffic. A day's delay in reaching the
ticket office nevertheless often means that no ticket is available. In an emergency
one must then seek more expensive transportation by air. These conditions are
not merely indications of density of population. They are also indications of rising incomes and standards of living. Travel is one of the most popular national
pastimes.

Land for dwellings in the great cities commands fabulous prices, and for
this reason much of the urban population is housed in quarters greatly smaller
and often otherwise inferior to the country homes they left behind. Japan has
sought relief for its housing problems principally by erecting apartments. Many
apartment houses have been built by private entrepreneurs, who usually offer tiny
apartments that would in other lands be regarded as slum dwellings. With the
principal exception of a few areas of Tokyo and Osaka, however, the word
"slum" is inappropriate. The attitudes and behavior of the residents of the
cramped quarters in congested neighborhoods is not that of slum residents, and
they would be shocked and offended to hear their dwellings referred to by this
term. They are instead self-respecting, law-abiding citizens forced by national circumstances into substandard housing. Among them are many people of middle
class and a growing number with college degrees.

An increasingly large part of the urban population is relying upon govern-
mentally financed housing. Great developments that consist principally of apartments, sometimes quartering as many as thirty thousand or more people, have
sprung up in all the major cities. Generally very small and, by Western standards, quite inadequate for domestic life, the apartments are nevertheless modern, hygienic dwellings with plumbing, and they are made available at moderate
rentals. The growth of these national housing developments and of privately-
owned apartments is recent, swift, and gaining added momentum. Prospects for
the future suggest that within a decade or two Japan will be a nation composed
principally of apartment dwellers. There is no returning to the country. The life-
line of Japan depends upon increased industrialization and urbanization—and
city life long ago became a value in itself, a way of life perceived as far superior
to grubbing in the soil or hauling in fishing nets.

It has been stated previously that the cultural changes in the past century
occurred under conditions of internal peace, but this statement does not imply a
lack of social disturbances. These have been ever-present, although they have not
reached the point of large-scale violence. Postwar trends of social change have,
however, prominently included sharp increases in crimes of violence and juvenile
delinquency, and the emergence of other social problems. Organized bands of
adult criminals, tied together by personal bonds of the *oyabun-kobun* tradition,
infest every city. Juvenile delinquency abounds in several varieties that include
young people who support themselves by crime, those who seek thrills through
crimes of violence, and those who find pleasure in their peers' company by taking
sleeping pills and cultivating bizarre fashions in clothing, and in music and other
forms of entertainment. Working mothers have brought to Japan the problem of
"key children," who must carry keys to the family house or apartment and whose
behavior and welfare are sources of worry during the times when no adults are

present to watch over them. Strikes of industrial workers and demonstrations of many kinds—by students, housewives, and various other groups—are common. These, it must be added, are not often accompanied by violence.

A putative general decline in moral standards is a matter of national concern, at least to the extent that it is frequently the subject of public expressions of alarm. Everywhere civic leaders plead for improved standards of morality, and they often refer to sexual morality. Almost any urban citizen of mature years will state that the family system has collapsed, that old values have disappeared, and that confusion reigns. But he generally makes these statements with composure, and it is evident that he has found a way to live with peace of mind.

The questions that suggest themselves are how have the modern Japanese rationalized their ways of life, and what are the modern values. The answers are far from clear, and they are ones in which the Japanese themselves are intensely interested. Sociological awareness has become part of the national commitment to science, and the nation—in the person of scholars and governmental bureaus—conducts unending research on attitudes and values. These studies clearly show that much of the old is gone. The studies provide no clear or systemic picture, however, of new values and ideals, which is hardly surprising in view of the continued change.

It is certain that part of the nation has sought aid in religion for the solution of its problems, and it is noteworthy that the religions in question are new, principally faiths that have arisen since World War II. Within the realm of religion great changes have also come about. The old, established religions of Shinto and Buddhism have remained essentially static in their teachings and practices and have lost their relevance for most of the nation. Weakened by diminishing incomes, many Shinto shrines and Buddhist temples have been forced to conduct festivals as commercial enterprises and to operate such outright money-making establishments as tearooms, day nurseries, and schools of flower arrangement. Buddhism is commonly referred to slightingly as the "graveyard religion" because most citizens come into contact with it only at times of funerals and memorial services. Shinto is seldom mentioned at all, perhaps in part because it evokes unpleasant memories of emperor worship associated with defeat and suffering in war. Once high, the social status of Buddhist priests is low, and many priests must take part-time employment in secular positions in order to subsist. Shinto priests are few, and the prospects for their replacement in the future seem dim. Noted shrines and temples see crowds of visitors, especially during festival seasons, but these visitors include many sightseers attracted by the ancient and famous buildings that have sometimes been officially designated as "national treasures" of architecture.

Although it has exerted considerable influence in other ways and especially through the educational and philanthropic endeavors that it has supported in Japan, Christianity has made little progress in gaining converts. Total membership in the numerous Christian sects totals only about seven hundred thousand persons, less than the membership of any one of a number of new Japanese religious sects that have risen to prominence since the end of World War II.

The most intensive religious activity of the nation is conducted by the so-called new religious sects, which are sometimes old in their teachings and often a doctrinal composite drawn from Buddhism, Shinto, and Christianity. These are religions that draw their adherents chiefly from the lower social strata. All have simple teachings and provide a sense of social identification by emphasizing active participation in the company of fellow members. They offer also the promise of faith to cure illness and bring recovery from other misfortunes. The total number of new sects formed and legally incorporated since the war's end is great. Some have been ephemeral, but over 150 survive. Most have memberships of only a few thousand persons, but a few have mushroomed to giant size and national importance. These large sects offer many added attractions, fine facilities for sports and the cultivation of music, painting, and other forms of aesthetics, and opportunities otherwise unparalleled in Japanese society for achieving positions of high status on the basis of individual efforts unconditioned by considerations of familial connections and other personal ties. Of the great new sects, Sōka Gakkai ("Value Creating Society"), a laymen's society of Nichiren Buddhism that extolls its faith as a recipe for worldly happiness and material prosperity, is the largest and most aggressive. Claiming in early 1965 a membership of more than thirteen million persons, a figure regarded by nonmembers as considerably exaggerated, Sōka Gakkai is well known throughout the nation. It is also feared and hated by many citizens because of its fierce intolerance of other religions, practices of forced conversion, stated aims of converting the nation and the world to Nichiren Buddhism, and, perhaps especially, because of its successful invasion of the Japanese political world.

Despite the feverish religious activity on the part of some sectors of the population, there has been no national revival of religion. The circumstances are to the contrary. The nation as a whole moves further and further from religion and meets the problems of life in secular ways. Public opinion polls show that approximately two-thirds of the population disclaims religious faith. A common response of Japanese citizens to questions regarding religious affiliation is to say that the "family" religion is one or another of the numerous sects of Buddhism. Further questioning reveals that the speaker himself has no religious faith. To most people religion is not a subject of interest.

Generally regarded as quite apart from the realm of religion are various supernaturalistic beliefs concerning good and bad luck. Although customarily called superstitions, these retain considerable life, and many citizens find nothing anomalous in referring to "true superstitions."

In the realm of secular life many of the old ideals and attitudes exist among people of all social strata. One should be faithful to his commitments, however much these might have changed. Thrift, industry, persistent struggles to success against heavy odds, and self-improvement in human skills and capabilities continue to be regarded as virtues. In combination they represent one of the most highly cherished Japanese values, the premium placed upon achievement. This Japanese value has sometimes been likened to the so-called "Protestant ethic" of the United States and northern Europe, and there are indeed close resemblances. Perhaps the most conspicuous differences are that the role of Japanese religions in reinforcing or engendering the ethic seems comparatively small and that, rather than cherishing work for its own sake, the Japanese people appear to value industry chiefly for the specific economic, social, and associated psychological rewards that it may bring. These words are not to say that the Japanese value lacks moral import. The lazy person in Japan is more than merely lazy; he is regarded as untrustworthy and morally unsound.

How the Japanese stress on achievement and industry as values might have come into existence is unclear but much in the conditions of life of the Tokugawa era may be seen as fostering it. Unremitting industry and thrift were then necessary for maintenance of the social order and necessary simply for survival in a land so poorly endowed in natural resources. As with human beings elsewhere, the Japanese population made virtues of the ways of life open to it. Mere poverty is, of course, an inadequate explanation of the emergence of the ideals in question. At best it provides only one environmental condition suitable for their growth. Examination of social and economic circumstances of the Tokugawa era suggests the nature of other stimuli. Under the conditions of the time, when the commoner and even the *samurai* ordinarily lived in bitter poverty, it is not difficult to see the relationship of thrift and industry to the other reigning values of filial piety and loyalty to superiors. These latter values depended upon the former and served strongly to reinforce them. It is not surprising that the *samurai*, who depended entirely upon their lords for small fixed stipends, should exalt frugality and loyalty to their lords to the status of virtues or that the rulers should champion the same ideals.

Thrift and industry were twin virtues that brought rewards beyond mere continued marginal existence to the rising merchant class of Tokugawa times. The merchants could amass wealth secretly, and through the power gained thereby could discreetly raise their social status by alliances with *samurai* families in desperate financial straits. After the end of the Tokugawa era the abolishment of sumptuary laws and relative freedom for social movement made concrete rewards of these desirable kinds easier to win. The amassing of wealth was generally possible, however, only through the practice of thrift and industry. To be sure, wealth was quickly accompanied by conspicuous consumption that marked achieved status, but even conspicuous consumption ordinarily demanded protracted thrift. The ethic of achievement has certainly seen no weakening in modern times. Perhaps the increased opportunities to achieve and to raise one's social status by one's own efforts have given it added strength.

Whatever the origin of this ideal, the modern Japanese "naturally" values industriousness and "naturally" wishes to succeed. He desires also the visible symbols of success in the form of material possessions. Self-denial of ordinary necessities of life in order to purchase at outrageous prices such objects as alligator handbags, imported suiting materials, Swiss watches, jewels, and Scotch whiskey is by no means exceptional. These are things that may be displayed—the Scotch whiskey in a glass case in the living room—and they reflect prestige upon the family or the individual. Rather than being the antithesis of thrift, they are most often in Japan another aspect of it, occasional rewards of thrift that bring great satisfaction. It is not difficult to think that the Japanese emphasis on hierarchy, whether by achievement or prescription, and its accompaniment of tangible symbols of status continue today to reinforce thrift and achievement as virtues.

The golden key to success is education, and plans for success are long-range. Improved economic conditions in recent years have made college degrees economically possible for a growing number of the nation's youth, but educational facilities cannot expand quickly enough to accommodate the aspirants. Competition to enter colleges is intense, and a large part of the applicants must presently be rejected. Planning for college often begins when children are infants, and competition to enter schools with favored reputations begins at the level of the kindergarten. In order to improve the prospects of their children for successful admission to a fine university, parents make strenuous efforts, selling their homes and moving if necessary, to secure for the children the best possible elementary and college preparatory educations. Schools specializing in cramming for college entrance exams abound in the major cities.

Other old values continue to exist without conspicuous change. Japan remains a society in which children are highly cherished and desired, and where, during the first years of life, children are treated with utmost indulgence. Physical aggression and the outward expression of anger continue to be strongly disfavored. The opinions of one's fellows remain a powerful force toward conformity, and identification with groups continues to be highly desired. But the obsequious follower and constant assenter finds no high favor today. Although the bonds of old custom often make this difficult, a growing sentiment holds that the individual may and even should assert himself if his motives are unselfish. Within the limits permitted by obligations, pleasure seeking continues to be approved, and the forms of pleasure and the time and money for indulging in them have greatly increased. Alcohol remains one of the pleasures for men and one of the societal safety valves, although national attitudes toward drunkenness are less tolerant than formerly. While under the influence of alcohol, one may still express emotions freely and indulge in other behavior that is ordinarily not acceptable. Crimes committed while under the influence of alcohol formerly brought little or no penalty. Legislation recently enacted makes inebriation no excuse for crimes and offenses against society, but the attitude of the courts and the general population toward drunkenness still tends to be lenient.

What seems radically new is the national attitude toward happiness. The pursuit of happiness, a concept that implies maintenance of moral standards and thus does not precisely coincide with pleasure, has become a worthwhile goal of life. Once viewed as an immoral doctrine that threatened the achievement of proper goals of fulfilling obligations, the quest of happiness is an ideal that has gained wide currency throughout the nation.

One of the characteristics of Japan that is perhaps trivial but lingers forcefully in foreign memories is still amply strong. Japan remains a land of bad odors. Sewage systems are poorly developed. Because the great Japanese cities attained large size long ago and lie in areas with poor drainage, the cost of installing sewage systems for whole cities is prohibitive. Night soil, used principally today for dry land crops rather than paddy rice, is collected by farmers and commercial collecting concerns. But circumstances that generate odors go beyond these and they relate to another Japanese cultural trait that impresses foreigners. Japanese feelings of responsibility toward public places and facilities remain poorly developed despite a sustained barrage of national urging to develop "public morality." Parks, streets, and other public places are heavily littered with trash. In preparation for the Olympics in 1964 government officials regarded it as necessary to conduct extensive campaigns to tidy up the nation before meeting the scrutiny and possible threat of unfavorable judgment of foreign visitors. Close kin to littering is the Japanese custom, confined usually to males, of urinating in public places. Almost any public place will serve, including the streets of downtown Tokyo after nightfall. Before the Olympics citizens of the whole nation were urged to cease urinating in the streets. But in this matter too Japan has changed. Odors are somewhat less prevalent than formerly, and a note of charm has been added. The postwar vacuum trucks that drain city toilets play tinkling music which brings to mind the ice cream vendors in the United States.

Related to these matters is still another subvariety of what the Japanese regard as public morality. In Western eyes Japanese behavior toward fellow citizens in public conveyances and other public places reaches grand heights of callous rudeness. National campaigns urge citizens to cultivate "transportation morality" by guarding places in queues and ceasing to push and buffet each other at train and subway stations. Japanese behavior in public places, toward unidentified members of society, contrasts sharply with the consideration and courtesy extended to those identifiable as members of one's own ingroups, and undoubtedly reflects the importance attached to group identification. Our account has made it clear that change is evident here also. The hue and cry about public morality indicates that at least part of the nation has come to hold new values. We may note also that some of the old etiquette of courtesy to be used in relations with identified members of society, whether inferior, equal, or superior, have been altered into forms of behavior that are simpler and more democratic.

The old coexists with the new, and the new is often a trend of change in which the old remains recognizable. Japanese society, for example, has not yet escaped the influence of paternalistic custom, and modern women of Japan have not yet attained to a status that even approaches that held by men. Other old attitudes concerning social superiority and inferiority retain considerable strength. Although many of the small Eta-like groups of near-outcasts vanished after their traditional occupations became obsolete in the twentieth century, such of these groups as remain identifiable today and the many modern communities of Eta constitute minority groups that continue to be the subjects of social discrimination.

To sum up, we may say that modern Japanese society has grown in diversity, in strata, and in substrata. There are indeed values that appear to permeate the whole, but at the same time Japanese culture is a kaleidoscope of ways of life that reflect differences associated with both social class and years of life. It is for this reason that the choice was made to describe the lives of both country and city people who represent the changing ways of three generations. The families about which I write are composites, and in this sense they are fictional. The circumstances and events of their lives that are here described are very real, drawn from personal observation and experiences of the author. Real communities have been chosen as the settings—a small rural settlement of southwestern Japan and the great industrial cities of Osaka and Tokyo. The rural community of Takashima is in fact as it is described, and it is inhabited by families bearing the surnames of Matsui and Otsuka. But no single family of Matsuis may be identified as the family described in the pages that follow. Sociological awareness has also reached rural Japan. Some of the residents of Takashima read and study anything that is written about their community. Because much of the account that follows is personal, it seems appropriate to disguise the characters to prevent identification and thus avoid the possibility of offending people for whom I have high regard and affection.

The Modernization of Japan— A Decade Later

As the preface to this revised edition notes, the changes occurring in Japan in the past ten years have been primarily further developments of trends well established a decade ago. As in the past, the prime mover has been economic growth, itself one of the trends of change.

For some years now Japan has ranked third among the nations of the world in gross national product. Achieving this position has entailed many changes in products and in modes of production toward increasing mechanization and the use of new techniques. These industrial innovations are sometimes foreign-derived but, as ever, they are molded in Japan in accord with native circumstances as well as the foreign market. Automobiles are small, to suit roads, resources of fuel, and pocketbooks, of other peoples as well as those at home. The cultivators, harvesters, threshers, combines, and other mechanical agricultural aids that have in recent years become standard equipment throughout Japan are miniatures, well suited for miniature farm plots. Where greatness of size is appropriate, as in ships for transport and for sale to foreign nations, Japan builds the largest in the world.

As Japan has continued its industrial growth and enlarged its foreign market, its self-sufficiency has progressively declined. More than any other large nation of the world, Japan depends for its well-being upon international well-being. As salesman to the world, Japan is also increasingly a prime customer in the buying of raw materials. These are not limited to metals, minerals, petroleum, fibers, and other industrial materials which Japan lacks. In accord with an international trend toward specialization in production, the imports include growing quantities of foodstuffs, luxuries as well as necessities, which other nations can produce more cheaply and efficiently than Japan. Of the staples important to the Japanese, rice is home-grown in adequate quantity as the result of developments in agronomy that wrest much food from little soil. Fish and other marine foods are also largely Japanese; that is, they are the result of Japanese gleanings in nearby and distant seas. Beef, pork, and wheat, which are consumed in growing quantities, must principally be imported, and even the supplies of such "oriental" foods as soy beans and rape-seed oil come mostly from the United States and Canada.

These are precarious conditions of existence, as the leaders of the nation and all knowledgeable citizens are well aware. Achieving and maintaining eminence in industrial production and international trade entails much knowledge of foreign affairs and the careful nurture of international relations. Newspapers and other news media of the nation give great coverage to international news, and Japanese diplomats as well as merchants are active everywhere. Increased national wealth has allowed the development of a program of foreign aid for underdeveloped nations that has escalated from modest beginnings to huge sums. Certainly not exclusively an act of humanitarianism, this program of foreign aid is doubtless motivated by prospects and hopes of reciprocal favors. Special attention is given to the economically developing nations of Southeast Asia and Africa, potentially great markets in which all industrialized nations have understandably keen interest.

Our concern here, however, is principally what has happened at home in Japan. The outsider seeing Japan after an absence of ten years quickly notes certain changes. Reflecting national prosperity, the streets, shops, and public facilities are cleaner and brighter, and many new buildings have been added. The luxury goods available in the many smart shops are more luxurious than ever. The streets and expanding network of highways are congested with motor vehicles of every kind, and these prominently include many privately owned automobiles. Consciousness of "public morality" appears to have grown. People in subway and surface train stations push each other somewhat less, maintain places in queues better, strew less litter. Men urinate in the streets less frequently than formerly, and the many pungent and often unpleasant odors of Japan have thinned. As in previous years, the urban air still contains many pollutants that soil clothing quickly, but governmental and public consciousness of the problems of environmental pollution has grown and remedial action is attempted.

The people in the streets, many of whom were well groomed in former times, are now often turned out handsomely. Male white-collar workers and businessmen, as ever, wear their badge of office, a neat uniform consisting of a suit of sober color, a white shirt, and a necktie of inconspicuous color and design. But other people are more adventuresome, and clothing of every kind known to the Western world is abundantly in view. In this matter as well as in other things, however, the old continues to be present. Middle-aged and aged women often continue to prefer the increasingly expensive clothing of Japanese style.

But the appearance of the people in the streets has come to differ in another way. The young are larger and taller than formerly, and their bodily proportions have changed. The growth in body size is now marked enough so that dwellings and furnishings, which generally preserve the dimensions prevailing in years long gone by, are often too small or too low for comfort. Teen-age sons and daughters often tower over their parents. Both sexes tend to have longer legs and thus proportionately shorter trunks than formerly, and young women have slimmer legs and larger bosoms.

These changes have a history of some decades of development that has accelerated in recent years. A main contributing factor is, of course, changes in diet toward increasing consumption of animal proteins and other body building foods and reduction in the consumption of starches. The new foods are costly ones which former incomes would generally not allow, and they are often in part imported foods. Changes in the proportionate lengths of legs and trunk are customarily explained by Japanese physicians and physical anthropologists as attributable to another cause with implications that are also economic, a change in custom associated with the industrialization of Japan. Few young Japanese today habitually sit in traditional style with folded legs, a custom which is said to have shortened the length of legs by obstructing circulation of the blood. Most young and many middle-aged people of today suffer discomfort when circumstances, such as attendance at funerals in private homes where chairs are not available, require them to maintain the traditional sitting posture for any length of time. Young women are often reluctant to sit in the traditional way for fear that doing so will result in unattractive legs.

As the visitor moves about the nation, other matters draw attention. The route of the famous superexpress trains had become doubled by 1975, extending from Tokyo to northern Kyushu. Other great construction projects are in progress or are planned, including mammoth bridges that will span the island-studded Inland Sea. Everywhere an atmosphere of relative prosperity prevails, and the dense crowds of travelers have become denser. Prepared foods available to the traveler are more Western than formerly, and thus more convenient, and the diet of young people in the large cities has come to include the provender supplied by the Japanese branches of McDonald's, A & W, Colonel Sanders, and Dunkin' Donuts.

A development that strikes the eyes through signs and advertisements, and the ears from listening to either casual or formal speech, is the evergrowing use of English words and expressions. From present indications, the Japanese vocabulary of a tomorrow near at hand will include English as a third large component, in addition to native Japanese words and a multitude of Chinese-derived terms that have been in use for many centuries. Like the Chinese words, the English terms are rendered with Japanese pronunciation and tend also to become further modified, especially by abbreviation. Following an old trend, English words often displace their Japanese equivalents. For example, a passport is now in the process of becoming a *passpōto* rather than a *ryoken* (Chinese derived), and the sizes of readymade clothing have for some time been labeled as "S, M, L and LL (extralarge)." Other new words are curious combinations of East and West. *Mantan*, "full tank," the standard term for a full tank of gasoline—and among children at least, sometimes the word for a full stomach—derives its first syllable from Chinese and its second from the English "tank."

Congestion in the cities of Japan grows ever more intense. Despite a low birth rate, legal abortions, and the use of effective practices of contraception, among which "the pill" and intrauterine devices are nationally prohibited as being injurious to the health, the population increases annually at a rate of over 1,000,000 persons, reaching 112,000,000 in 1975. The old trend of demographic shift from rural areas to urban, industrial centers continues; about 60 percent of the national population lives in urban areas. Farming prefectures continue to lose population and industrial areas to gain, but the growth of the largest cities tends to be at their peripheries. These are the places where immigrants can most easily find newly built living quarters which they can afford, and they are also attractive to old urbanites who have grown weary of the discomforts of life within the hearts of the cities. Within its incorporated boundaries, Tokyo has shrunk slightly in population, but in fact it continues to grow as a metropolitan area and retains its position as the world's largest city. A counter trend, probably old but only recently noted and as yet not a strong development, consists of moving back to small home towns after some years of urban life. This tendency, called in Japanese the "U-turn" (*yūtan*), is most common among the advanced middle-aged who have retired from industrial employment. However, since urban employment is often available to residents of nominally rural communities, even young people sometimes return. This trend should not be understood as being prompted solely by nostalgic yearning for simple, backwoods life. Rural areas have shared in national changes and the old home town is now often better described as a country place or a suburb, within quick reach of a city or within a city.

As the demographic shift implies, the farm population of the nation continues to shrink. Converted into full-time equivalents, the proportion of the labor force engaging in agriculture is well below 10 percent. Imminent crisis has plagued agriculture for decades but has never yet become actual crisis. As the years have passed, farming has increasingly become part-time work carried out by men employed full or part time in industry, their wives, and their aged parents. Technological innovations, especially in the form of farm machinery, have temporarily averted the crisis of a shortage of labor, and they have at the same time allowed the farm population to shrink further. Much of today's farming is in fact physically an urban activity, since the growth of cities has led to the construction of houses and commercial buildings in what was formerly farmland so that, more than in the past, farmland and urban structures intertwine. At least at its peripheries, any industrial city of Japan is a seemingly nonurban aggregation of rice paddy and dry farm plots interspersed with factories, business offices, apartments, and houses.

During the past century the farmers of Japan have probably been by far the largest category of living representatives of the Japanese ideals of thrift, industry, sobriety, and the drive to achieve, but circumstances of the past seldom allowed them to become prosperous. Today, the farmers and part-time farmers are economically well favored, a condition which few of them had ever expected. Nearly 90 percent of the farmers also have nonagricultural employment; their farm produce brings high prices, and their land has large and mounting value. The average incomes of farm families exceed the average for the nation, and the educational levels of farm children similarly surpass the national average for their age group. The new-rich farmer is common, and he has often gained much of his wealth by selling a part of his land at a great price for some urban enterprise such as an apartment or business office, a practice which was formerly not permissible, or by using his land himself to become an urban entrepreneur.

The looming crisis in agriculture concerns the children of farmers. Very few of the maturing sons and daughters of farm families intend to live by farming, an occupation regarded as humble and which, in any case, does not require full-time labor. Most will go to college and later follow the specialized occupations for which their college training suits them. Like other near crises, this threat will probably be met by technological changes that will require an even smaller labor force and make farming more and more a part-time occupation. No land reform that might allow large-scale farming has yet been seriously considered, and how the future heirs to farms will handle their property is unclear. At present, few people are willing to sell more than a small part of their holdings of land.

Trends of change in social relations and social organization have also continued along the paths of earlier years. The family continues to shrink somewhat in size, averaging 3.72 persons in 1973, but the ideal family still consists of two parents, one son, and one daughter. A son is still often preferred as the first-born child. The tendency of aged people to live apart from their children grows, fostered by increased wealth and by an accompanying sentiment among the aged themselves that doing so is proper and preferable. An eldest son who is oya-tsuki, an expression meaning that his parents are "attached" or "stuck" to him, is often handicapped in finding a bride. Few young women care to face the prospect of living with and caring for long-lived parents-in-law for spans of time that may reach decades. Governmental surveys indicate that most middle-aged parents intend to live apart from their children when they are aged. These reports often refer to this trend as an "alienation of the generations," but since emotional ties between parents and adult children often continue to be close, it seems more appropriate to describe these circumstances as separate residence without true alienation. The nuclear or conjugal family is thus both preferred and most common. Concomitantly, families in the nation are not only smaller than formerly but also proportionately as well as absolutely much more numerous.

Within the small family, relations are still intimate, and familism in attenuated form is still evident in a number of ways. Among these are the paternalism that is still evident in relations between superiors and inferiors in the business world and the nature of Japanese labor unions, which will later be discussed. Familistic attitudes are also evident in other contexts, such as the Japanese expression "family suicide," used when a man kills his wife and children and then commits suicide himself. Familism is explicitly questioned from time to time, however, as in a recent court case which contended that the Japanese law providing a heavier penalty for killing one's parents than for the murder of other people is undemocratic and therefore unconstitutional. As this matter now stands, the law regarding parricide has not been rescinded, but it has been questioned before the eyes of the nation.

In the realm of social structure and social relations, the trend continues toward a growth of horizontal or egalitarian lines of organization and a softening of vertical lines of authority or hierarchy. The most striking growth has been in common-interest associations, which reflect the specialization that characterizes industrial societies. Labor unions have grown in number, size, and power. Totaling about 64,000 in 1975, the labor unions continue to be principally industry based; that is, a firm has its own union. Some occupational unity comes through pyramidal national federations of unions based upon types of work, and several such federations embrace most of the individual company unions. No overall unity of labor exists, however, because each union looks upon itself and its company as a familylike group and gives principal regard to its own interests. On the federation level, unions are often rivals, sometimes resorting to violence in their rivalry.

The mass media of communication give extensive coverage to the activities of the labor unions and other associations, such as a national teachers' union and, of course, the nation's political parties. Demonstrations and strikes by labor unions are commonplace. Demonstrations sometimes concern political matters, but since the unions present no united front, they have so far never acquired national importance in politics.

Even the world of crime continues to be organized into associations, although the several hundreds of these groups in the nation tend to be much more familistic and hierarchic in their organization than other associations, in which egalitarianism ideally prevails. No sizeable city of the nation lacks organized groups of criminals, which, like the labor unions, have tended to embrace larger areas and to form the equivalents of union federations.

Beyond these newsworthy associations is a vast number of others that receive less or no publicity because they concern avocations that are regarded as harmless or desirable. These are voluntary associations centered on sports, games, esthetic pursuits, hobbies, and other activities of leisure time. Especially outstanding among these are the *kurabbu*, from the English "club," associated with and paternalistically supported by industrial firms. A large firm may have a dozen or more of these organizations centering on various sports, hobbies such as flower arranging and the tea ceremony, and educational activities such as the learning of English. The firms will ordinarily gladly sponsor additional clubs upon receiving from employees requests to do so, which are usually transmitted through the labor unions.

Although seldom so regarded in popular thought, religious sects are also appropriately classifiable as common-interest associations. In the past decade, the "new" religious sects of Japan, those which were established or first rose to prominence in the 1950s, have lost much of their novelty, are quiet, and do not often make news. Even Sōka Gakkai, the largest, most assertive, and most powerful of the new sects, seems to have entered the sobriety of early middle age. Other developments in religious affairs throughout the nation superficially suggest a renascence of religion, particularly of Buddhism. Sales have boomed of *Butsudan*, Buddhist votary altars that are kept in homes, and of headstones for graves; funerals are often grand affairs, and visitors at Buddhist temples and Shinto shrines are plentiful. Rather than evidence of heightened religiosity, these events appear to be reflections of economic well-being. Most of the nation's citizens continue to disclaim religious affiliation with any organized religious sect. ▪

Hierarchy continues to prevail in politics, business, the family, male-female relations, and elsewhere, of course, but there are many signs of continued, gradual change. Notable among these are the present customs of marriage and male-female relations of authority. Dating couples are still more frequently evident than formerly, and the trend toward choosing one's partner in marriage appears to be on a growing course. Once the choice is made by the principals, however, the traditional procedure is still customarily followed; that is, use is then made of a go-between, whose role now consists only of making the formal arrangements of marriage. The present ways of finding husbands and wives include both the old and the new principles, of selection by persons other than the bride and groom, and of self-choice by the bride and groom, and they appear to be a fortunate combination for current times. Those who wish and are able to meet and socialize with potential mates may generally make their own choice. For those who are socially or psychologically inept in contacts with members of the opposite sex or who lack opportunities to meet suitable persons, the old procedure of using a go-between to find mates is still available. Parental consent has usually become a foregone conclusion.

The status of women remains well below that of men, but the breach appears to have grown smaller. Eighty percent of the able-bodied, adult females of the nation are gainfully employed, full or part time, and females are thus economically important. The number of females attending college is only very slightly below that of males, and women have slowly entered some of the occupations once reserved for men. Included among these occupations is crime; the rate of crimes committed by women has grown annually at a low rate for some years. The women's lib movement is active if not militant, and occasionally women take a firm stand to combat discrimination. A successful court case in 1974 charged that illegal discrimination was involved in the practice of a radio and television broadcasting company of retiring female employees at age thirty. As the age distribution of the nation's population has shifted toward a greater proportion of old people, instances of female dominance also seem to have increased. Many aged women clearly appear to dominate their husbands, a state that seems to be common in many parts of the world and is probably old also in Japan.

Discrimination continues against the two small minority groups of the nation, the Koreans and the Japanese outcasts, the *tokushu burakumin*, "residents of the special hamlets," a euphemistic term usually abbreviated to *burakumin*. The outcasts are also known by a number of additional names including the term *eta*, used in the original edition of this book. Although acceptable in scholarly writings, this term has a strongly demeaning connotation and is seldom spoken or used in other contexts. The lot of the minority groups has surely improved somewhat, however, and they actively pursue their causes through their associations, taking legal action from time to time. A murder committed in 1963 by a member of the outcast minority group has become one of the famous crimes of the century because of the legal and popular contention relating to the outcast status of the convicted murderer which the event evoked. An appeal to mitigate the sentence of life imprisonment heard in late 1974 claimed forced confession and discriminatory treatment because of the social status of the accused. The appeal was denied, but the case appears to be far from dead. Court action initiated by the associations of outcasts charging discrimination in policies of hiring among employers of the nation has resulted in legislation resembling the Equal Opportunity laws of the United States. The outcasts nevertheless continue to be the subjects of discrimination, hold the least desirable types of employment, have the lowest levels of education, and have the highest crime rates.

Many of the statements of the preceding paragraphs have been accounts of onward and upward movement. Still other statements of the same kind may be made. National educational attainments certainly forge upward, and Japan stands next to the United States in the number of its high school graduates presently going on to college. Compulsory education is still limited to nine years, but nearly all young people continue their formal education beyond that point. Sanctions for doing so are powerful. Year by year the kinds of employment available to young people have depended increasingly upon their educational attainments. For young people with nine years of schooling, a condition that has come to imply some sort of deficiency of intelligence or character, only the least desirable kinds of work are available. Science, literature, and the arts also forge onward, so that Nobel laureates have ceased to be a rarity among the Japanese.

In repetition of past history, the many changes described here have entailed no serious social disturbances. The most outstanding social disruptions of the period were uprisings among college students, sometimes violent, which struck all institutions in varying degree in the late 1960s. As with their counterparts in the United States and elsewhere in the world, no clear or satisfactory explanation of the reasons for the disturbances has ever been offered, and the campuses returned to peace after a few years.

But, of course, serenity, progress, and prosperity have not applied to all aspects of national and private life. Small social problems of many kinds exist, and several large problems have arisen or loom on the horizon. Politicians continue to be involved in scandals and labor unions to conduct inconveniencing strikes, but these are conditions that have long been endemic and can be taken in stride. Small firms continue to go bankrupt as competition from enlarging firms becomes more intense; but this also is an old story, and small firms are still important nationally. Crime is endemic, of course, and although national crime rates have generally declined in recent years, a small tendency toward increased juvenile delinquency and, as noted, an increase in the incidence of crimes by women are somewhat worrisome. A relatively high divorce rate and instances of women abandoning their husbands and children are also worrisome. The problems related to the nation's two minority groups are a minor worry from the viewpoint of the nation as a whole because the number of minority group members is small, two to three percent of the population.

Traffic accidents are a great threat to life, but this hazard is taken for granted and many safeguards have been devised that have lowered the rate of accidents in recent years. Among these is the imposition of severe penalties for drunken driving. For the average citizen, international economic and political circumstances are acknowledged to be a great problem, but they are more or less shadowy matters about which he generally feels powerless to act.

The large, immediate problems intimately concern everyday life, and all of these are in some degree economic problems. The entire nation is concerned over threats of an economic recession and problems of galloping inflation, which proceeds at a rate that currently offsets the rises in individual incomes of the past year or two. But this problem is also in part international and beyond competent solution by ordinary citizens. Associated with and intensified by inflation is another sorely vexing problem that has now beset Japan for many years, a shortage of housing or of adequate housing. Life in the crowded *danchi*, the public and private housing developments, or in cramped private apartments and houses grows more and more tiresome. For many people, no way to escape is available. Costs of land, building materials, and labor have risen monumentally, so that even high incomes often do not allow the purchase of houses or the rental of desirable quarters. Young unmarried men, who live for perhaps one-tenth of their salaries in the company *danchi*, which each large company must provide as a fringe benefit for its employees, can afford to buy cars and otherwise to spend money freely. Young married men who, following the national trend of attitude, wish to live away from the *danchi* and thus also away from the eternal shadow of their employers, are generally troubled financially. They must often settle for living quarters that are poorer and much more expensive than those of the *danchi*. The combination of inflation, the national shortage of land suitable for dwelling sites, and the shrinking of the size of the family together with the concomitant increase in the number of individual households have had one curious result. The average farmer or other resident of a small community who has inherited a sizeable house lives today in quarters that, with or without the aid of remodeling to modernize them, are far more spacious and luxurious than the homes of most urban residents.

Environmental pollution, another great national problem with a long history of existence, was formerly taken for granted. Rising to much greater heights of severity as industrialization progressed, it forcefully entered consciousness as a problem that must be solved. Smoke, noise, and the presence of human and industrial wastes in bodies of water had been the order of the day for many years in the great industrial cities of Tokyo and Osaka. New technology and the spread of industry brought all of these and still more noxious pollutants to many other cities. Sickness and death from gases, mercury, cadmium, and other modern industrial effluents then set into action a movement toward remedy. The problem was then given a name, *kōgai*, "public damage," which became well known to all citizens several years ago. *Kōgai* refers only to sickness, death, injury, and financial loss or other damage as the result of man-made alterations of the environment. The names of several cities in which distress arising from these causes has been particularly acute, such as Kawasaki, Yokkaichi, Fuji, and Minamata, have become synonymous with the term *kōgai*. Labor unions, fishermen's and farmers' cooperatives, citizens' associations of other kinds, and municipal, prefectural, and national agencies all clamored for alleviation of the problem. Environmental pollution is still acute, but many legal statutes now regulate relevant activities of industrial firms, and these firms have often been required to make compensatory payments to citizens.

One additional problem is not yet severe, but the prospects for the future are threatening in manifold ways. As this problem is generally regarded today, it consists of devising ways to care for the aged people of the nation, but there is growing awareness that the problems have many facets and are not simply a matter of providing for the indigent aged. Like other current social problems of Japan, the problems associated with the lengthening of the human lifespan are shared by other technologically advanced nations of the world. More than elsewhere, however, the difficulties appear to have entered the consciousness of the Japanese, perhaps principally because Japan's version of the complex of problems developed with great speed. Among nations of the West, the lengthening of average lifespans was a gradual development over a period of many years. In Japan, most of the lengthening occurred in the last two decades, and therefore it took the nation by surprise. Advances in medicine and improved conditions of life in other respects have lengthened the Japanese life expectancy to a span somewhat greater than that of citizens of the United States. As in the United States, women live several years longer than men. Expectations are that lifespans will continue to lengthen and that the proportion of aged people in the population—in 1973, 7.5 percent were 65 or more years of age—will soon be much larger. The economic and other problems of the aged population of Japan are complicated by the general practice among industrial firms of retiring employees at age 55. A traditional countertrend also exists, but does little to alleviate the problem since the number of people involved is small. Heads of business firms and other people in very high positions do not ordinarily retire at age 55 and tend to be older than their counterparts in Western nations.

Present activities toward meeting the problems of the aged consist principally of expressions of concern, attempts at fact finding, and exhortations to take action in the form of legislation of social welfare to aid the needy.

Despite the stresses that face most of the nation, no slackening is evident in the pursuit of happiness by people of any age, provided, of course, that obligations have first been met. A national trend toward shortening the work week to five days has given more time to many people, and greater incomes have enlarged the arenas of pursuit. Old avocations continue, and new and expensive hobbies have developed. For the middle-aged and the aged, the most popular current hobby is the cultivation on a large scale of flowering plants, notably potted chrysanthemums and azaleas, a hobby which few people could previously afford. The young have a huge list of Western and native hobbies, sports, and other forms of entertainment. Almost everybody travels, going as far as the generally prudent use of incomes will allow. The aged visit temples and shrines, nearby or far away in accord with their pocketbooks, and, more than formerly, they are able to visit their children in other communities. The young, and their seniors who are financially favored, travel everywhere. Within their own nation, they now often travel by private car, and thus the new roadside motels, which generally rent rooms by the hour, have taken some of the clientele from the "short rest" inns of the entertainment areas of the cities. Guam is a popular place for honeymooners, and if enough money is available, Hawaii and still more distant points are more desirable.

This account has been one of developmental change. No other portrayal would be reasonable or accurate. It is useful to note again that change has not meant a revolutionary sweeping away of the old. Something else seems especially worthy of note, and it also is a continuation of the past. The overall atmosphere in Japan continues to create an impression of calmness and adjustability, of active but never explosive ferment. From an historical viewpoint, the innovations of the past decade are simply another segment in a long series of alterations that have proceeded at a rapid pace without leading to internal collapse or chaos. The successful adjustment of the people of Takashima to drastic changes in their lives, as described in Part 4, is a specific version of one series of events in the chain. Just as the people of this small community adjusted swiftly and without disorder, so one gets the impression that the nation as a whole will accommodate itself without critical distress to the problems it now faces.

2

A Rural Family

Introduction

THE SEACOAST of Okayama Prefecture bordering the Inland Sea is a place of exquisite natural beauty, where rice fields and pine-clad hills meet the calmest sea dotted with myriad islands. A mild climate and moderate rainfall make it a region suited for year-round activities outdoors. It is a place for vacation excursions by Japanese families of nearby cities and for growing numbers of tourists from more distant places. A popular tour sponsored by the Japan Travel Bureau takes Japanese and foreign tourists to a resthouse atop a hill in Kojima, a city of eighty thousand people, from which the islands of the Inland Sea make a picture postcard before them.

Like many other rural cities of Japan, Kojima is a loose collection of formerly independent farming, fishing, and industrial settlements that amalgamated for reasons of administrative economy and efficiency. The city's primary industry is the manufacture of school uniforms, and about 40 percent of the nation's annual production of these garments comes from its factories. Between some of the city's residential areas lie extensive paddy fields and a small range of forested hills. Travel between the scattered parts of the city is ordinarily by means of buses that make frequent runs.

Kojima is the home of the Matsui family, which lives in the *buraku* of Takashima, "High Island," a small settlement separated from its nearest neighbor, Shionasu, by a distance of about a quarter mile. Officially a part of Kojima since 1948, Takashima is in some ways still an independent rural community. Its population in 1965 was two hundred persons in thirty-six households, somewhat over half of which derive their livelihood from fishing augmented by small-scale farming. The main occupation of second greatest importance is farming. Several household heads have recently turned from fishing and farming to work as unskilled or semiskilled laborers in nearby industrial plants. One household head is a trained civil engineer. Three unmarried girls and one widow work as clerks and

34

employees of clothing factories in Ajino, the largest community of Kojima, which lies about three miles from Takashima. Once an island, Takashima is now a low hill of approximately thirty acres. Its dwellings cluster in two segments separated by a small graveyard and occupy only a few acres. Community facilities include a newly built harbor for the fishing boats that consists of stoutly built breakwater piers of concrete, and a community hall. A small building of one room with reed-matted floor, the community hall is used principally as a place to conduct *buraku* business meetings. During festival seasons and on other special occasions, the hall is also regularly used by young people as a scene for playing games, and it sees occasional further use for serving refreshments to any large group of people. Several community wells from which community residents draw water by pump or bucket are scattered through the *buraku*. Only two religious edifices are ordinarily regarded as communal property. The more important of these is the shrine to the tutelary god, a small houselike structure of one room beneath the pines at the top of the hill. A miniature shrine at the harbor is also looked upon as communal. Scattered about are various small stone figures of supernatural beings and miniature shrines, put in their places by persons and for reasons now forgotten. No one feels responsible for the care of these objects, but someone sees that they receive token offerings on the appropriate ritual occasions. The rest of the land pertaining to the community consists of dry farm plots, privately owned, and small stands of pines. Some of the farm plots have been recently abandoned and are overgrown with grasses, shrubs, and seedling pines. Once communally owned, most of the pine forest is the property of the National Forest Service. *Buraku* people still make some communal use of the forest in gathering fallen needles and branches for firewood.*

The ways of life of Takashima stem from a farming rather than a fishing tradition. The community did not turn to fishing as an important means of gaining livelihood until nearly a century ago, and its people take pride in not being ordinary fishermen. Customs and attitudes of the community differ in no marked way from those of neighboring farming settlements, with whom the people of Takashima share schools and other public facilities and intermingle freely. As residents of a community that specializes most heavily in fishing, the residents of Takashima do not have high social status, for in Japan fishing has generally never held high esteem as an occupation.* A Takashima man or woman who distinguishes himself in enterprise or in any other desirable way suffers no loss of premium, however, because of identification with his community.

In this respect the people of Takashima differ from the residents of Hama, one of their neighboring *buraku*. The people of Hama are "special" fishermen with whom ordinary farmers, fishermen, and tradesmen mingle only to the extent demanded by the activities of the public schools and ordinary economic and civic affairs. Once impoverished, migratory fishermen who lived on their boats, the Hama people were pariahs, "a half step above the Eta."* Despite leading lives today that are not discernibly different from those of their neighbors, they continue to hold this outcaste status. Their neighbors call them Sokobiki, "Bottom Trawler," a name taken from their technique of fishing, but this term has such base connotations that it is ordinarily used only among intimate acquaintances and is sometimes whispered. The use of this word within the hearing of a resident of Hama would be a gross insult. The Hama people are in fact no longer fishermen. In the early 1960s they were forced to give up this occupation because dredging of the ocean took away their fishing waters, and they then turned principally to wage labor in industrial plants. Takashima residents share the prevailing attitudes toward the people of Hama. Individuals among the Hama people may be held in good regard for special abilities or traits of character, but the group is beyond the pale. Marriage to a Sokobiki is ordinarily a disgrace and occurs only rarely, when some unfortunate person is "led astray by money." As neighbors separated by a distance of less than a half mile, residents of the two communities inevitably have a variety of contacts. Relations are cordial, but the people of Takashima strictly avoid any social contacts that suggest intimacy or equality.

Takashima ceased to be an island in 1963. Land dredged from the bottom of the sea to form a deep ships' channel for new industrial plants in nearby areas was dumped off Takashima's shores, making it part of the mainland and creating a large plot of land suitable for industrial plants. By 1963 a large oil refinery and a plastics factory had been erected nearby in the adjacent rural city of Kurashiki on land similarly created. Plans called for the erection beginning in 1965 of a cement factory and other industrial plants in Takashima's former sea channel. Fishing and farming are surely doomed, but Takashima will doubtless retain many characteristics of a rural community for some years to come. Its residents say that in the matter of its future their *buraku* does not differ from hundreds of other small communities throughout the nation, whose young men have gone to the large cities and whose household heads commute to industrial work in nearby cities, leaving the farm tasks to their wives and aged parents.

Takashima fishing is netting, done in nearby waters from small motored boats, and is an enterprise of individual families. Fish are caught principally by long floating gill nets in which the fish entangle themselves and drown. A minimum of two persons is required to handle the boat and nets. A man and wife combination has become the most common working force, as many households lack two able-bodied males. Farming is principally the cultivation of vegetables and fruits in plots that average about a quarter acre for fishing families. Full-time farmers cultivate holdings of about two acres. Some fishing families raise vegetables for cash sale, onions, radishes, carrots, Chinese cabbage, giant radish, and chili peppers. A few families own small rice paddies in a community a half mile from their own. Agriculture is principally for home consumption but, as such, it is important to the livelihood of the people. Among fishing families, farming is regarded as the work of women. Increasingly it is the work of the aged women, even among families that specialize in farming, for the number of men who work in industry grows year by year.

By local standards few Takashima households are poor, and two or three are rich. Most households congratulate themselves on their economic well-being as compared with former times. They state with pride that every family has a television set, an electric washing machine, and various smaller electric appliances, and that half the families have refrigerators and piped water, supplied from wells by small electric pumps. These are all great luxuries almost unknown in the community until the mid-1950s. Most families have planned their domestic finance to allow for the purchase of similar, added luxuries in the foreseeable future.

Community life on Takashima is intimate, more intimate than many of its present-day residents would like it to be. Most people are somehow related to each other, occasionally many times over, and they customarily address by kin terms all persons who are their seniors in age whether or not a relationship exists. The dwellings, thin-walled inside and outside and separated from each other only by narrow, winding pathways, impose further intimacy. Under these conditions the rubbings of daily social life produce irritations. Covert ill feelings are common enough and subtly communicated, but communal peace must be maintained and successful efforts are made to preserve amicable relations. Community life presents an unruffled exterior marred only uncommonly by harsh exchanges of words and outspoken disagreement or disapproval. Tolerance of others is the mode, but memories are known to be long, and the behavior of any person is continually open to the inspection and unspoken judgment of all. Channels of gossip are exceedingly swift and efficient, so that one must watch his own conduct carefully and exercise great caution in passing judgment on others. The newcomer, who is almost always a bride coming into the community at the time of marriage, is under especially close surveillance. Since the bride often lacks relatives or close relatives in the community except her husband and his kin, she may be discussed more freely than others.

Increasing contacts with outside communities have broadened the social worlds of Takashima's people, making the small pains of intimacy both more endurable and consciously less desirable. The enlarged and changing world has at the same time given birth to new attitudes that sometimes conflict with the old. Perhaps now more than in the past tolerance is needed, even among those with the strongest ties of affection and dependence. Grandparents, parents, and children live in different worlds that tolerance reconciles, permitting the family and the community to carry on.

The Family Members

Hajime, "First Born Son," age 44, is the head of his household. His surname of Matsui is shared by most of his neighbors and is therefore little used within the community. His wife, Hanako, "Flower Child," is five years his junior and the mother of two surviving sons and one daughter. Another son, their third child, died in infancy of a disease finally diagnosed as poliomyelitis after his death and the death of two other children in the *buraku*. The last child, a son, came much later, after familial economic circumstances had improved.

In the interval between the birth of her third and fourth children, Hanako had undergone a surgical abortion performed by a physician in Ajino. This was done with the full knowledge and approval of her husband and his parents. Many of her neighbors had undergone similar surgery. No shame was involved;

the operations were lawful, and no real attempt was made to keep them secret. For the first two children Hanako had the services of a trained midwife before and at the time of their birth. The birth of Makoto had promised to be more difficult, and, at the advice of the midwife, a physician trained in obstetrics had been consulted during the eighth month and had officiated at parturition. The pregnancy had been frightening to Hanako because the midwife had darkly pronounced that there was some possibility of twins. The idea of the work and expense entailed by twins was of course worrisome, but the really disturbing things were the unnaturalness of plural birth and the accompanying feelings of shame. There were no twins in the community and none had ever been raised there. Some had been born but were given out in adoption, with some difficulty and always separately. Hanako told no one of her problem and had considered having another abortion. The obstetrician had said that her fears were unfounded, but she remained apprehensive until the birth took place. Hanako herself and Hajime had been born with only the ministrations of a *buraku* grandmother with long experience in attendance at childbed.

There had been some troubling moments during the infancy of all the children, when Hanako had been reluctant to follow the old customs that grandmother made ready to carry out. She had been unwilling to give the newborn infants the traditional infusion of bitter herbs that grandmother had in readiness, but she had finally pretended to do so. Many other old customs had been circumvented in the same way without giving offense to grandmother. Some of the customs surrounding pregnancy and childbirth were, of course, very simple to follow as well as being absurd. Hanako did not find it difficult during pregnancy to observe such taboos as those against eating octopus, lest her child be born boneless, or eating misshapen vegetables, lest the child be similarly misshapen. Grandmother had seen to it that the placenta and the bath water used at childbirth had been properly buried in the ground beneath the floor of the room where birth took place. She had also carefully wrapped the umbilici of the infants in cloth and paper and tucked them away in a drawer for possible future use of which even she was ignorant. Out of deference to grandmother, Hanako had tried to remember to avoid other people for thirty-three days after childbirth, but this had been a trying and impractical custom. She had also tried to remember to sprinkle herself and the house with purifying salt when the prescribed period had ended. Grandmother spoke of making a "new fire" at this time, as she also had at the end of the mourning period when the great grandparents had died. But a new fire was built as a matter of course every day, and this old custom that grandmother attempted to follow had no meaning for Hanako.

The rearing of the children had thus followed practices that combined tradition and innovation. When the children were ready for weaning at about two years of age, Hanako had followed the practice common when she was a child. Rubbing the juice of freshly broken chili peppers on her nipples had brought dramatically quick results. In other matters of child rearing Hanako had leaned self-consciously toward the new. Well aware of theories of nutrition from lectures she had heard by visiting specialists in public health and from reading articles in women's magazines, she watched the children's diet with care. After the death of their third-born child, she had not hesitated to consult a physician when symptoms of illness were evident. After the national program of socialized medicine reached Takashima, there had been no economic reason for failing to seek trained medical counsel. The children were healthy and all were so large that she habitually purchased for them clothing intended for children two years older than their actual ages. None of her children had ever had physical punishment, and if sometimes troublesome in early childhood, at least the elder two were now obedient and well mannered.

The eldest child is named Akira, "Brightness." At age sixteen he is a sturdy young man five feet eight inches in height, four inches taller than his father. His sister Yuriko, "Lily Child," fourteen, is the same height as her father and towers above her diminutive mother and grandparents. Akira attends high school and Yuriko junior high school in Ajino. Makoto, "Sincerity," is a lusty boy of five years that old people often guess to be seven or eight.

Hajime's father, sixty-nine, and his mother, sixty-five, complete the human members of the household. For all ordinary purposes these old people have no given names. Beginning with Akira's birth their names had gradually become "grandfather" and "grandmother." Four years earlier, when Hajime had assumed the position of head of the household at his father's expressed wish, his parents had already become grandfather and grandmother to most people of the community except their peers in age. Following the usage of their children, Hajime and his wife have also come to refer to them and address them by these names. Hajime and Hanako also often call each other "father" and "mother," especially when the children are present.

Hajime and Hanako are second cousins who were only casually acquainted before their marriage. Hanako was the daughter of a farming family of Yobimatsu, also a community of Kojima city, and she and Hajime had seen each other now and then as children. Their marriage had been arranged by neighbor Kotomi, now a spry grandmother, whose skill as a go-between had then been recognized for more than ten years. Kotomi, delighting in her fame, described her services as a humanitarian duty. She served without fee beyond a gift from the parents of the young men and women whom she united; took the utmost care to see that prospective brides and grooms were suited to each other in all important ways; and took second place to her husband in the seating arrangements at weddings that she alone had arranged. The marriages she brought about were rarely failures, and she could point to the union of Hajime and Hanako as one of the successes. During the New Year's season Hajime and Hanako unfailingly made a formal call at her house, bringing a small gift as an expression of thanks. Kotomi and her husband are benefactors in other ways, for which additional debts of gratitude are owing. At the naming ceremonies conducted for Akira, Yuriko, and Makoto seven days after their birth, these two had served as name giving godparents and they have since that time maintained a special interest in their protégés.

Grandfather and grandmother are also regarded as second cousins, but grandmother was adopted in infancy by a childless couple of the community and her genetic relationship to grandfather is remote. The identity of grandmother's genetic parents had not been kept secret from her, but she did not maintain contact with them and for decades now has hardly given them a thought.

Grandfather and grandmother had no such benefactors at marriage as Kotomi and her husband. Married long ago in a day when life on Takashima was bitterly impoverished and lacking in most social graces, their marriage, like that of many of their contemporaries, had been of a different sort. It had been a marriage of mutual attraction, a "free marriage," and the union was marked by the offices of only a token go-between, called in at the end, and the simplest and most inexpensive of festivities. Other people of greater wealth and higher social status of the time married in the proper way with genuine go-betweens, bridal gifts to the parents of the bride and groom, and elaborate feasts, and they preferred not to think of the somewhat shameful way in which they had become man and wife. They had seen to it that their son Hajime had had a proper marriage, replete with all formalities, including a gift of money to the bride's parents in token payment for losing her. Although the wedding came not long after the end of the war when household finances were yet a little troublesome, by dint of earlier sacrifices the wedding feast had been a grand one. Outside caterers had been called in to supply and help prepare the food, and the banquet was crowned by the serving of several large, golden-red *tai,* the most highly prized and expensive of fish that symbolizes good fortune and is especially well suited for a wedding feast. Their daughter-in-law's parents had also contributed their full share. Hanako came with a good dowry of clothing and household equipment, and in her fine *kimono* and bridal wig, she had been a fitting bride at the wedding ceremony and feast.

Using the privilege of frank speech given to men of his age, grandfather sometimes makes jokes about the marriage customs of Takashima and Japan. According to him, the *buraku* and the whole nation have now reverted to the old days of savagery when the natives married for love. Everyone recognizes these statements as a joke. The young people of Takashima know about love marriages in the cities and think about romantic love. Unless they migrate alone to faraway cities, their marriages are arranged through their parents, who are usually careful to have the full consent of their children. Only the old men and women of the community like grandfather and grandmother, and only those whose families had been very poor, had selected their own spouses.

Nonhuman members of Hajime's household are a stub-tailed tomcat called Whitey, and four chickens, confined in a pen beside the house. The chickens also have names, derived from their characteristics or histories: Elder Sister, who dominates the others; Spot, a speckled dowager; the One from the Main House; and Number Four, the latest addition. These are all cherished members of the family. Elder Sister and her companions provide eggs and fertilizer, but the idea of killing and eating them is unthinkable. When chicken is eaten, it must come from elsewhere. Many predecessors of the present small flock have died of old age and been buried.

According to the custom of the community, everything animate and inanimate that pertains to the household is commonly referred to by other community members as "'Hajime's." Thus grandfather is Hajime's grandfather; the cat is Hajime's cat; and the household fishing boat is Hajime's boat. Hajime and all other members of his family refer to each other and to family possessions from the point of reference of the family as a unit, "the grandfather of our family," and "our family's cat." A few Takashima households still bear house names acquired in times long gone by. Only one, Rice House, the name of a well-to-do family that long ago raised rice for sale to other community members, is in frequent use today.

Hajime's family is historically but no longer functionally a branch family of Rice House, established five generations earlier for a second son of the time. During the passage of over a century since the branch house was established, its ties with the main house have thinned. The present household heads are distant cousins, a relationship they do not bother to trace precisely. The once intimate and economically important ties between the two houses have essentially disappeared, and the present families are for ordinary purposes neighbors rather than relatives. Hajime's grandfather and grandmother still make formal calls at Rice House during the New Year's season and they customarily speak of it as "the main house." Hajime's children seldom use this term. Their contemporaries in the community would not ordinarily understand such a reference.

Hajime was born in Takashima, as were his father and mother. As the eldest son and heir, he began life as a favored child. He would inherit the position of household head, continue in the traditional occupation, and support his parents when they became aged. One of five children, Hajime alone of his siblings remains on Takashima. His three sisters, all younger than he, had married in due course and gone to live with their husbands in other communities within a radius of ten miles. Now and then the sisters come to visit, but as the years have passed, their visits become less frequent. The oldest, busy with affairs of her children, her husband, and her in-laws, has not visited Takashima for two years. Another member of the former family, Hajime's younger brother, Jiro, has not returned to Takashima for three years, and little news has come from him during this time.

Family Life

Hajime's family lives in an ordinary house. One enters it through a small yard of hard-packed sandy soil. A clump of flowers—cosmos, chrysanthemums, and other easily cultivated plants—brightens a small corner of the yard. Other ornaments include a camellia bush and other shrubs, growing apathetically in the sandy soil, a flourishing and well-tended fig tree, and several pottery jars once used, like lobster pots, for catching a species of small octopus. Attractively encrusted with barnacles, these are placed together before a large, rough stone. Most of the space in the yard is bare, for the yard must serve as a place for doing household tasks and work connected with the fishing nets.

Rich families of the *buraku* have houses with two stories, but Hajime's is the more common kind with a single story that forms a rectangle. The house, built forty years ago after a fire had destroyed its predecessor, is of wood, with a partially timbered exterior that is plastered with a mixture consisting principally of clay and straw. The roof is gray tile. The several houses erected in the community within the last few years have metal roofs, which are less expensive and said to be just as good. Two very old houses have thatch roofs, but these are now regarded as the mark of poverty, and their owners find it more troublesome year by year to engage specialists capable of repairing them.

The customary entrance to the house is near one end, through an entrance room that serves also as a storage room for fishing and farming equipment and many other things. A votary shelf honoring the tutelary god of the community is attached to the wall in one corner. The floor is concrete, laid only two years earlier to replace the packed earthen floor that had been traditional for centuries. Beneath the floor lies an old storage bin for sweet potatoes, which had to be laboriously filled with sand from the beach so that concrete could be laid. Sweet potatoes, a cheap food and once a mainstay of the diet, had then ceased to be a necessity. After some debate the family had decided that the merits of a smooth, unbroken concrete floor outweighed the economic value that the storage bin represented. Since that time most of the farm land that had been devoted to sweet potatoes has been used for watermelons and mandarin oranges, which grandfather looks upon as wild extravagances.

A doorway in an immovable wooden partition leads from the entrance room into the kitchen. Also concrete-floored, the kitchen contains cooking equipment, foodstuffs, a small electric washing machine, a wooden table for preparing food, and a small sink and cold water tap that were installed at the time the concrete floor was laid. Food is served on a low table on a raised wooden platform at the side of the kitchen adjoining the sleeping rooms. The diners sit on the floor. Hajime and his wife sometimes talk of replacing the platform and low table with a more modern high table and benches or chairs. Out of deference to grandfather, whose legs hurt when he sits in a chair for a long period, they have decided to wait.

A wood-burning earthenware stove stands out prominently in the kitchen. Intended primarily for steaming rice and used also for cooking other foods that might be steamed, boiled, or deep fried, it was rendered nearly obsolete in 1960 by an electric rice steamer of shiny aluminum alloy. The stove is seldom used now except during the festival seasons when much food is prepared, and during the coldest weather, when the heat radiating from it is comforting to Hajime's wife and grandmother. In addition to the electric rice steamer, a portable charcoal brazier, a new kerosene cooker accommodating one cooking pan, and an electric hot plate for use when time is pressing are the customary cooking equipment. No foods are baked and no equipment for baking is owned. Hajime's wife sometimes talks of buying one of the new portable ovens that may be placed on the kerosene cooker.

To the Western eye the kitchen is rude, dark, and not very clean. To Hajime's wife and especially to grandmother, who have given much of their lives to raking the pinewoods for twigs and branches for firewood and homemade charcoal, to fanning reluctant fires, and to carrying water from a community well, the kitchen is a place of efficient luxury. The floor of the forest, immaculately clean until about 1958, now bears a carpet of pine needles, and passage through it is impeded by small fallen branches. The charcoal is generally purchased today. Some women even speak of its use as troublesome, preferring the kerosene stoves and electric hot plates unless an elaborate meal is planned.

Four additional rooms with elevated floors lie to the left of the entrance room and the kitchen, and are accessible from them. According to the views of the community, the house has four rooms, as the kitchen and entrance room are only appendixes to the house proper. From the standpoint of their primary functions, these four rooms are a living room, a room for entertaining guests, and two sleeping rooms. All rooms are used for sleeping when guests arrive.

These four rooms are tidy and clean. Entry to them is ordinarily through the entrance room by means of a benchlike step. Sliding partitions of wood and paper separate the rooms. If the partitions are removed, a rectangular floor space of approximately 18 feet by 22 feet is created. The house affords no true privacy. One may be out of sight of others, but he is never out of the range of hearing, and it is sometimes convenient not to see and not to hear. Floors of the room are covered with expensive reed matting that soils and scuffs easily. Footgear must be removed in the entrance room.

Furnishings are simple. The small living room contains only a seldom-used radio, a much-used television set with a ten-inch screen, and, attached to the wall, a small votary shelf in honor of the household gods. When the children wish to do written schoolwork in this room, a low table is brought in from the adjoining reception room. The reception room, the finest and largest room in the house, contains a low table around which cushions are placed for sitting. A recessed alcove, which forms the center of beauty of the house, contains a painted scroll and, when flowers and time for arranging them are available, a floral arrangement. Walls are decorated here and there in this and other rooms with small framed pictures of Swiss lakes and famous Japanese scenic views.

The sleeping room used by Hajime, his wife, and Makoto contains a miniature dresser with moveable mirror, a large chest of drawers, a storage chest, and a new electric sewing machine. The adjoining sleeping room, adjacent to the kitchen, has another chest of drawers and an elaborate, lacquered Butsudan, where the household ancestors are enshrined. Bedding consists of thick quilts stuffed with cotton batting, which serve as mattresses and blankets, narrow cotton sheets, and tiny pillows, the older ones stuffed with husks of grain and the newer with cotton or synthetic fibers. These are stored when not in use in closets with sliding doors in the reception room and bedrooms. Each family member has his own bed. Akira and Yuriko have slept in separate rooms since Akira reached the age of nine, Akira in the living room and Yuriko in a bedroom.

Illumination comes from an electric light of low wattage suspended in the center of each room and fitted with a shade only in the reception room. No heat is provided or regarded as necessary most of the year. Snow is a rarity and the temperature sinks to freezing point only a few times at the height of winter. The most important protection against cold is clothing. As winter advances, additional and warmer clothes are donned, and long underwear is a standard part of men's garb for several months of the year. Most clothing is Western, but grandmother always wears traditional garb when it is time to dress up and Hanako usually does so when she leaves the community or when guests come. Hanako does not dislike Western clothes, but short skirts are uncomfortably cold in the winter months and she feels that with advancing age the less revealing contours and rich fabrics of native *kimono* are more becoming to her. What is more, all her contemporaries dress as she does. When working, grandmother and Hanako often wear trouserlike *mompei,* which are comfortable and warm. Large white aprons are a standard part of their workaday garb. Grandfather and Hajime own old Japanese clothing, purchased when they were young men, and Yuriko owns Japanese clothes only recently purchased. These are reserved for very special occasions. Akira and Makoto have no Japanese clothing except outgrown garments used in their infancy.

Many days and nights of winter are too cold for comfort even when bundled in warmest clothing. During these times a charcoal brazier containing a few glowing coals serves to warm the hands. A wooden frame is sometimes placed over the brazier and topped with a quilt. Those who crave warmth may then sit on the floor, place their feet and legs under the frame and tuck the quilt around their bodies. Metal containers filled with hot water are used to warm beds. Among the recent additions to household equipment is an electrical equivalent of the brazier and frame. This is ordinarily used only for guests and on the coldest evenings when Akira and Yuriko do homework. Best of all for fighting evening cold is a hot bath.

Grandfather and grandmother sleep in a bedroom in a separate small building that flanks the main house and also contains a storage room. This separated bedroom is their place of refuge when they tire or when the children become excessively noisy. Before grandfather's retirement from the position of household head, they had both for several years looked forward to the occasion, to the peace and quiet that relinquished responsibility and moving into the secluded sleeping quarters would give them.

Other appurtenances of the house are the bath and toilet, both in a separate structure near the dwelling. Neither bath nor toilet has running water, but a new cold water tap is near the bath so that the conical cast-iron tub may be filled with water easily. Wealthier homes have wooden bathtubs, which are said to have a nice feel and are popular. A few new houses have more expensive baths, built to order, of tile recessed below the floor. The cast-iron tubs have become a little small for the large bodies of the modern young men, but they are thrifty of water and fuel. Water is heated by burning firewood beneath the tub. Painful burns from the heated bottom of the tub are avoided by a wooden lidlike float that the bather pushes with his feet beneath the water to a point where it lodges. The toilet contains a porcelain urinal attached to the wall which male members of the family are careful to use, for the home is a hallowed place and not like the public streets. Another porcelain fixture was recently added to the toilet and serves principally to outline a narrow rectangular opening in the wooden floor over which one squats. Akira likes to keep magazines in the toilet for diversion, and he must sometimes be asked to leave.

Beneath the toilet opening is a large earthenware receptacle for the wastes. The contents of the receptacle are removed from time to time and placed with added water in similar containers in the farm plot. After a period of aging, the nightsoil is applied by bucket and ladle to the growing crops. When the nightsoil is allowed to remain in the receptacles for some days, it becomes relatively odorless. Exigencies of the working schedule do not always allow the full time for aging, and fields and houses are sometimes blanketed with stench, to which everyone is accustomed. Hanako sometimes talks tentatively of abandoning the use of nightsoil in favor of the exclusive use of chemical fertilizers, but agrees with her husband that this action is for the world of tomorrow. There is truth in his statement that, although unpleasant for grandmother and her to handle, the nightsoil must be disposed of in some way and it is a costless fertilizer.

Daily Life

Household life begins early in the morning. Hanako is the first to rise, at five or six in the morning. During the heavy mackerel fishing season in the late spring, she rises still earlier. She is usually soon joined by grandmother, whom she often reminds that such early rising is not necessary. The two prepare and set on the dining table a breakfast of steamed rice, slices of pickled radish, soup made with bean paste to which a little onion and sometimes small pieces of fish are added, and green Japanese tea. Rather frequently now, boiled or fried eggs are also a part of the breakfast. When grandfather sees the eggs he sometimes looks puzzled, consults his failing memory, and asks what festival day it is. Sometimes, when he looks at the rice, he expresses concern over household finances. During most of his life rice was mixed with cheaper and less tasty barley for all except holiday meals.

Other foods that grandfather views with suspicion appear with varying regularity. Akira, Yuriko, and especially Makoto like boiled oatmeal with milk and sugar. Yuriko has herself several times prepared toasted bread and butter or margarine that she had first eaten while on a school excursion to Kyoto. All three children like to drink milk, which, in small quantities, became a standard part of the household diet after Makoto was weaned at age two. Milk is for the children alone. Grandfather could not be induced to drink it.

Yuriko experiments with new foods that she reads about in magazines or sees advertised on television. She once brought home a can of strawberry jam, which everyone agreed was a success. Only recently she brought a package of cornflakes, which proved a failure with everyone except Yuriko. She had insisted they were delicious, but the package remains on the shelf half full.

The family rises in an order that is fairly constant. After Hanako and grandmother come Hajime and, not always predictably, grandfather. Yuriko follows tardily, and Akira must be reminded several times that day has come. Makoto arises when he pleases, usually quickly after his mother. Yuriko helps in the morning work by folding and storing her parents', Makoto's, and her own bedding. She seldom has time to tidy her brother's room because he is so late in rising.

Meals are ordinarily not a time for much conversation. All eat quickly, and the men eat noisily. Akira's appetite seems insatiable, and he sometimes eats four full bowls of rice. The two women eat last.

Once the heaviest meal of the day, the noon meal is now often simple except at times when school is not in session. Noodles or left-over rice, hot bean soup, and cooked vegetables are its principal dishes. The main meal is now usually in the evening, when grandfather, Hajime, Akira, Yuriko, and Makoto—served in that order—eat together. Western and Japanese vegetables are served boiled and seasoned, together with the customary soup, rice, pickles and tea. An important part of the menu is broiled or boiled fish, served in small quantities four or five times weekly. Grandfather and grandmother have not yet become accustomed to this frequent serving of fish. Both remember a lifetime that ended only a few years ago during which good fish was for the rich and for special occasions. Takashima fishermen sold their fish, keeping only those damaged by the nets or by sharks and the few specimens of small, bony fish they had caught that had no market value. Animal protein came principally from clams and other shellfish with low market prices that the women formerly dug from the beaches daily at low tide.

Dependent upon the season, the occasion, and the amount of time available, numerous other foods are prepared. *Tempura*—vegetables, fish, and shellfish dipped in batter and fried in deep fat—is a favorite. Pork, fried in small strips or larger cutlets, and beef *sukiyaki* are special treats that reach the table a few times yearly. Festival seasons see fine foods and special traditional dishes of many other kinds. Confections are always on hand, to be served to guests with tea.

Fruit of every kind is greatly favored, but has only recently come to hold any importance in the menu. The children are especially fond of bananas, and they are served at Obon and New Year's. Other fruits are more common but still luxuries. The family takes great pleasure in the mandarin oranges and watermelons recently added to its crops. Between-meal snacks are customary. These are frequently boiled or deep-fried sweet potatoes, a food of very low social prestige which many people associate with the bad years just after the end of World War II.

After breakfast has ended much work remains to be done before the main tasks of the day begin. There are lunches to prepare for the children; the kitchen and bedrooms must be tidied, and preparations made for the day's work of fishing. Hanako and grandmother have worked together for so many years that all their actions are smoothly geared and little needs to be said. Mothers-in-law were by tradition often stern and critical mistresses, who found countless ways to criticize and dominate new brides. If differences arose between bride and mother-in-law, tradition demanded that the groom side with his mother. The bride then had no effective recourse, and rebellion on her part led to added criticism and sternness on the part of the mother-in-law. There had been such mothers-in-law on Takashima, and even now there are a few of that "feudal" sort. But Hajime's mother had not been that kind. There were of course stiffness and strain at first but grandmother had never criticized by word, look, or other action. Instead, she had found ready excuses when Hanako, in her initial state of apprehension, did things clumsily or improperly. Mother quickly became a source of comfort rather than fear, and she gave herself devotedly to the care of the children when they came. In her present role as grandmother she remains a beloved friend.

Activities for the day vary with the season of the year. Hanako is charged with responsibility for running the household and raising crops, and she also serves as her husband's assistant on the fishing boat. The load of tasks is great and she realizes that the burden of the farming is gradually being shifted principally to grandmother, who never complains. Grandmother is strong and in full possession of all her faculties, still capable of doing the farming and running the house efficiently alone. But this is not appropriate. She has retired and she deserves the freedom from responsibility that comes with retirement. A solution is available for the problem of farming. Since the income from fishing is now adequate to meet their needs, more land can be planted with mandarin orange trees, which do not need unremitting care. If necessary, still more of the least productive farm land can be abandoned, but grandmother is reluctant to do this as she takes pride in the cash that comes from the sale of the chili peppers she raises.

Work for Hanako has grown rather than diminished. In former days there had been enough men in the community to handle the fishing boats and nets, and only seldom did the women serve in fishing. In various neighboring communities of fishermen, custom until the war's end had prohibited women from entering fishing boats because of the baleful influences emanating from them. This custom did not become firmly established in Takashima, but fishing has never been regarded as women's work. The newly added plumbing, the washing machine, and other appliances help Hanako a great deal. The problem is not so much the intensity of the work. Her tasks are lighter than in former times, and there are many periods of leisure during the day, especially while on the fishing boat. The problem is how to make ends meet for lack of time to do the marketing, cooking, washing, housecleaning, sewing, and also fishing. It is, of course, a little shameful for women to fish, but life as a whole is far more pleasant than it formerly was and Hanako knows that her present lot is only temporary. When Akira and Yuriko have grown older there will be more leisure time. Even now there is free time much of the year in the off-season from fishing and on stormy days when no fishing is possible. Yuriko helps a little and, during the spring and summer school vacations, Akira is also helpful.

Grandmother finds her tasks rewarding and not onerous. The washing machine, the tapped water, the kerosene stove, and all the other innovations have altered her life. The bent back of grandmothers of earlier times is not her lot. She stands erect and is secure in her position as a wife, mother, and grandmother of a creditable and cherished family. There are worries, but these she can face. Grandfather is failing, at times quite childish, and she will have to spend her final years without him. This is the lot of grandmothers. She is aware of all the problems of other members of the family, but these are things that will be solved. She can do her bit by working and by requesting divine help to solve them.

Grandfather and the children are charged with few tasks. Grandfather tries to help with the fishing nets, but he tires quickly and he is often more of a hindrance than a help. He cannot see well, mislays his glasses, and frequently mis-

mends the nets. Farm work, except during planting and harvest, is beneath his dignity as a male fisherman. Intermittently dozing, he spends much time watching television, and sometimes he amuses little Makoto. He may then slip back to his own childhood, recounting the tales he had heard from his grandfather, spine-chilling stories of ghosts and demons. From grandfather, Makoto has learned that Jimmu Tenno, the first emperor of Japan, once lived on Takashima and that his ghost may be seen on moonlit nights walking the sands of Uragahama beach. Grandfather, and sometimes grandmother and Hanako, tell Makoto other tales that are less frightening but no less interesting—of the peach boy who sprang from the seed of a peach; the boy who went on a turtle's back to a fairyland at the bottom of the sea; and of the *kappa,* creatures both froglike and boylike that live in streams. *Kappa* can lure people and horses into the water, but once tilted so that the liquid in the concave depressions at the top of their heads is spilled, they are powerless.

Akira helps his father in fishing during the spring and summer school vacations and sometimes on weekends. He is strong and quick, and already almost as skillful as a mature man. Yuriko helps with dishes, laundry, and other housework, as well as regularly folding the bedding in the morning. She is talented at keeping Makoto amused and out of trouble, but she soon tires of his company. Hajime and Hanako are glad and proud that Akira and Yuriko will have high school educations. Their own schooling ended with the completion of the six years of elementary school required by law at the time of their youth. They are also proud that they never keep the children home from school to help with domestic tasks and fishing as so many families of the community felt obliged to do at various times in the past. A lesser evil that was common in Hajime's and Hanako's school days has also been avoided and has almost disappeared from the community. Neither Akira nor Yuriko has ever been a "baby-tender student," one who takes to school a brother or sister of preschool age.

Little Makoto, holding the least nominal authority, is unquestionably the most highly privileged member of the household. Within the limits of propriety, physical safety, and domestic finance, his wishes are indulged. The time will come soon enough when he will be introduced to rules of behavior that are less indulgent. Makoto will start kindergarten in April, the beginning of the school year, and he will then begin to learn the ways of responsible people. Meanwhile he is a child, without good sense, and he can enjoy his freedom. Temper tantrums are embarrassing when observed by others, but they are natural to little boys, and Makoto has had very few. Akira had been worse, especially after Yuriko's birth, when he had felt deposed and neglected. Akira had then often tried to push Yuriko from his mother's lap, which everyone regarded as natural behavior requiring no action but unstern urging to stop. Akira had gone further. He took to quarreling with the neighbors' children and had twice gone so far as to strike his playmates. Firm action was necessary for this terrible offense. He was reprimanded in the most serious tones by his father as well as his mother and told of the shame he was bringing on the family. Temper tantrums followed soon afterwards, and grandfather had then said several times that it was time for *okyū,* the tinder of powdered sage leaves that is burned on the skin to cure aches and pains and to punish fretful children. Grandfather's back still bears tiny scars from repeated treatments in childhood. Hajime had suffered *okyū* only once but had often been threatened with its use. The treatments and threats had brought about miraculous changes in their behavior. *Okyū* has never been given to Akira and Makoto, and grandmother, if not grandfather, knows that it is just another of the many outdated customs. On the rare occasions when the older children are unruly they can usually be brought into line quickly by calling upon their sense of honor and shame.

As the principal earner and head of the household, Hajime bears many responsibilities. Fishing and caring for the family boat and nets take most of his working time. The fishing season gets off to a busy start in late spring, when the mackerel are running. Then, for over a month, there is little time for sleep because the mackerel run represents nearly half of the year's earnings. The rest of the year is more leisurely, and fishing drops nearly to a standstill in the winter months. This is the time to overhaul the boat and the nets thoroughly. The nets, for the past several years made of nylon that does not rot or break easily, are efficient and easy to care for; but they need repair and careful handling if they are to last and bring a good livelihood. Hajime makes his own nets in the winter months, aided by Hanako and grandmother.

The boat is expensive, and it also requires care. Twice a year Hajime hauls the boat onto the shore with the help of neighbors and treats its bottom with coal tar and smoke from a fire of green wood to discourage barnacles and kill marine worms. When this is done he is careful to place a gangplank from the boat to the sand to allow the God of the Boat to leave, tapping the side of the boat with a stick as a signal for the god to disembark and to embark again when the treatment is finished. Hajime is uncertain whether the god is male or female or what other characteristics it might have. Some say the god has the form of a snake and some say it resembles a human female. Most do not know and have little interest in learning what its form might be. All agree that the god resides in the center of the boat and that it protects the boat and its passengers. Hajime does not wholly believe there is a God of the Boat, but this is old custom and following it is simple and comfortable. Many tales are told by older men of the disastrous consequences of failing to treat the god with courtesy.

A representative day of ordinary fishing takes Hajime and his wife ten miles from Takashima, on a sea that is calm or only slightly rippled. Many types of fishing require that they remain on the sea overnight as several species of fish may be caught only in the darkness. These are the times that Hajime likes the best. Soft breezes blow in even the hottest weather of full summer, and the sea is a field of twinkling lights from the boats of fellow fishermen with their hundreds of yards of nets floating by means of plastic buoys to which flickering lamps are attached. Freight boats and the occasional passenger ship expertly work their way through the fishing craft.

Meals are prepared on the boat and these may be eaten leisurely, for there is little to do while the gill nets are in the water. Sometimes Hajime and Hanako fish with hand lines off the side of the boat in hope of catching a fresh fish for their meal. Fishing boats with young men among their crews provide music from transistor radios, but even the progressive jazz that often comes from them seems muted and peaceful. Hajime and Hanako take turns sleeping on the deck, for someone should always be awake to avoid mishap. Until Makoto was weaned at the age of two, he often accompanied them. Special care was then taken to see that he did not fall overboard. Like most people of their age in Takashima, Hanako cannot swim and Hajime can hardly do so.

‘ Waiting for the harvest of fish is a time of peace and contentment, a time of freedom. As a youth Hajime had never been eager to become a fisherman, but he had grown accustomed to it. During the four years that he had spent in military service in China, he had come to long for his former life. Those years as a private and, finally, as a corporal had been long and trying, an ordeal of military discipline of the harshest kind. Beyond the initial novelty of army life and of life in China, there was little to remember with pleasure. His departure for military service had been rousing. All members of the community had been there to see him off, and the Women's Association had given him a warm woolen girdle to which each woman contributed her prayers for his welfare by knitting stitches. His return had been unheralded, and he did not care to recall the several years that followed, years of poverty and little hope, years of eking out an existence with threadbare clothing and the poorest of foods, a monotonus and skimpy succession of meals consisting chiefly of boiled sweet potatoes and barley. Then there had been the dizzying inflation that soon followed. In a single day of mackerel fishing he could earn the former income of a whole year, but the new income bought so little. The savings policy of seven hundred *yen* that his parents had maintained for fifteen years in expectation of paying all the expenses of his youngest sister's wedding had been barely enough to buy her a pair of wooden sandals of medium quality. All these were things that Hajime had successfully thrust from his memory years before. War, everyone agreed, was no way to solve the nation's problems.

The hardest but most interesting work of the family fishing comes with dawn when the nets are drawn in by hand, a task that takes up to two or three hours depending upon the number of fish caught in the net. When the net has been drawn and the fish placed in the holds, the motor is started and the boat proceeds as quickly as possible to the market of the Fishermen's Cooperative, four miles from Takashima. The fish are sold, a process that takes only a short time since prices are fixed and there is no question of bargaining. Hajime and Hanako then set off for home.

Hajime turns all funds over to his wife except a little pocket money for cigarettes and coins for the pay telephone at the Fishermen's Cooperative at Shimotsui. When he is delayed for long periods, it is sometimes convenient to send messages home by means of the neighbors, in whose house a pay telephone for community use was installed a few years earlier. No major expenditures beyond the customary are made by his wife without consulting him. His wife is thrifty and sensible and he almost always agrees with her suggestions. Hanako is, in fact, far more thrifty than Hajime, who sometimes worries about appearing stingy. He inclines to spend money lavishly when gifts are required and for food and drink for guests. In these matters he has learned to follow Hanako's more conservative judgments. The household budget is thoroughly planned to take account of these and other expenses, and a growing part of the income is set aside for deposit in savings accounts. Grandfather has regular pocket money, and grandmother seldom seems to want or need money except when she makes her short pilgrimages to shrines and temples. The children are always given spending money during the great holiday seasons.

Hajime's responsibilities and tasks do not end with the work of fishing. He must also look after the welfare of all members of his household and he has important duties to perform for the community. Free hours during the normal day and many days of the slack season find him busy with civic duties for the common welfare.

The Leisure Hours

Life is full of work, but it also allows much leisure. Even Hanako, who is charged with a greater variety of tasks than anyone else, finds time for pleasurable activities. Each family member has his own forms of entertainment and recreation, but many are joint. The most important of the joint pleasures for the past several years has been watching television. When the television set was first purchased in 1961, it was the cause of family discord. Akira and Yuriko neglected their schoolwork and quarreled over choice of programs. All that was solved by mutual agreement. Akira and Yuriko may watch when their schoolwork is done, and they have compromised with each other and grandfather on the choice of programs.

Grandfather and all his male descendants including Makoto like *chambara,* stirring dramas of the bold adventures and honorable exploits of ancient feudal lords and their retainers. When these are broadcast, the women of the household usually find other things to do. Makoto favors animated cartoons. Among his favorites are "Atomu," which concerns the adventures of a miraculous boy of the atom age named Atom; "Tetsujin," featuring a robot of the space age; "Popeye," and a variety of other American cartoons. Yuriko and her mother and grandmother like modern and period plays with Japanese themes in which rivers of tears flow. These Akira and Hajime frequently watch but deny liking. Everybody except grandfather and Makoto like the rebroadcasts of "I Love Lucy," "Rawhide," and the ancient Our Gang comedies, which have Japanese dialogue dubbed in. Akira and Yuriko agree in liking old American movies. The channel that broadcasts educational programs sees little use. As a result of television, bedtime is often later than usual by an hour or two; Akira sometimes does not go to bed until nearly eleven o'clock.

Grandfather rests much of the time, and puffs at a little old-fashioned pipe that holds only a pinch of tobacco. He seldom leaves the house or yard. Grandmother also rests when she tires, and finds time to talk with other women of the community. In former times she met other women when she drew water at one of the community wells. This had been a time for leisurely chatting and, if none of the wrong women were present, for interesting gossip. It is harder for her now to keep track of doings in the community, but news of importance reaches her quickly enough. Grandmother, joined by Hanako, also takes pleasure in cultivating the little plot of flowers. It is their privilege to pick select bouquets for friends from time to time. Grandmother finds it pleasant to amuse Makoto, and when he becomes cross or tiresome, she usually feels free to retire to her own quarters, where he understands that he should not ordinarily go without invitation. When grandmother takes Makoto with her to shrines and temples in the surrounding area, he still sometimes asks to be carried on her back but he has grown much too large. Grandmother transported all her children and grandchildren this way, in a kind of cloth harness, but the custom finds no favor with Hanako, who secretly thinks of it as a mark of low social class.

Hanako has women's tasks that are pleasures. She enjoys sewing clothes for her daughter. Yuriko wears her drab school uniform of navy blue most of the time, and she is always happy to don prettier and more colorful clothing, Western or Japanese. Her greatest pleasure is the few occasions in the year when she appears in fine Japanese clothing. Japanese *kimono* are far too precious, costly, and impractical for daily use but every girl must have at least one fine outfit for gala occasions. Hanako observes that Yuriko does not walk properly in the *kimono,* toeing out instead of toeing in. This is the habit of all the modern girls, because they wear Western shoes much of the time.

Hanako also likes to prepare and serve fine foods during the holiday seasons. Like grandmother, she finds time for talk and gossip with other women. She is active in the Parent-Teachers' Association and in the Agricultural Cooperative, which provide opportunities for pleasurable association with a wide range of friends and acquaintances. Shopping that takes her to Ajino and occasionally to Kurashiki City becomes an all-day excursion that has recently come to include lunch or, at least, a snack in a restaurant. When Makoto accompanies her, they sometimes drink Coca-Cola or eat ice cream, but she herself prefers a pot of tea.

Best of all for Hanako are the pleasures she shares with the other members of the family. These include the annual three-day visit to the famous Kompira shrine across the Inland Sea on Shikoku, when they take with them foods prepared beforehand at home, and now, year by year, supplement this food increasingly by meals in restaurants at the port of Marugame. Last year instead of sleeping on the boat in the old way, they stayed at a small inn recommended by their neighbors and that had been pleasant. Sometime during the trip they make a brief visit to the shrine and obtain wooden talismans that are added to the great collection at home from previous years. Most of their time goes to other activities, shopping, sightseeing, and resting.

Hajime also combines work with pleasure. He is active in the Community Association and in the Fishermen's Cooperative. Meetings of these associations and his work with his boat and nets afford many opportunities to talk with other men. Hajime drinks a little on festive occasions. He flushes very quickly when he drinks, which embarrasses him on all occasions except wedding feasts. Then he drinks more than a little and, uninhibited by his scarlet face, vigorously leads the singing and dancing. He knows many songs and has a powerful voice, and he is usually urged by others to begin the merrymaking. Hajime likes best to drink hot rice wine, and he is a little disappointed at its displacement by beer. Beer is good, too, but in his mind it cannot replace hot *sake* at a rich feast. Like his wife, Hajime enjoys most such group activities as wedding feasts and the more frequent occasions when his family and other relatives celebrate together.

Hajime's family is pleased that he is not one of the community gamblers, who play cards as if it were a disease, hiding from their kin to do so, and squandering their winnings on beer and other treats for their equally guilty comrades. Philandering with other women is both beyond Hajime's interests and pocketbook. There is no lack of professionally willing women in the larger nearby communities, but, except for two occasions in his youth, such women have been outside his world. These events had both happened during the autumn festival, and they had been joint excursions of several young men, all rendered adventuresome by festival alcohol. A few mature men in the *buraku* now occasionally patronize such women, Hajime knows, but no one regards such behavior as commendable and it holds no attraction for Hajime. These are, to be sure, only trivial offenses for which there is no condemnation by the other men or by the community, but wives of such men are pitied and lose face. If their husbands' behavior becomes known to them, some of the wives would not hesitate to complain.

The lives of Akira and Yuriko revolve mainly about school and the ordinary amusements of the young, which everyone regards as proper. There will be ample time later for the more serious considerations of life. Akira plays baseball at school and has learned a little about football and soccer. At home there is no open space large enough for baseball, but he and other boys in the *buraku* sometimes practice batting and pitching with their own baseball equipment in the road between Takashima and Shionasu. Sometimes he plays *go*, Japanese checkers, with grandfather or with other boys. He is an avid reader of the sports section of the newspaper and of science fiction magazines. He also collects postage stamps, but not many come his way and his album has many unfilled pages. Sometimes he plays ping-pong at the *buraku* public hall. He is a new member of the Young People's Association, which combines aims of providing recreation for its members with activities for the welfare of the community.

In the summer, when he is not out helping with the family fishing, Akira likes to go swimming, a sport that only recently became popular among Takashima boys. The harbor is a good place to swim and there are other unpopulated beaches nearby; but it is much more fun now and then to take the bus three miles to Shimotsui where interesting tourists throng the beach. There he may sometimes see with his own eyes things that he knows from television and the movies, beautiful sport cars and girls wearing bikinis.

Except for school events and a few activities of the Young People's Association, Akira's recreation is taken almost exclusively in the company of other boys. He has learned the facts of life, a little from chance observation in his own home and from casual remarks by outspoken grandfathers, a little more from schoolbooks and magazines, and much that is none too accurate from other boys. He knows very well that dating is common in the cities, but he feels uncomfortable in the presence of girls and thinks that the embarrassment of dating would be greater than the pleasure.

The most interesting time of the year for Akira is the annual school sightseeing trip. Trips of previous years have taken him to many places including the famous cities of Kyoto and Nara, and in his senior year the class will go to Tokyo. He enjoys the inns, even though they pack in as many students as the floors will hold bedding. Sleep comes late and is fitful, but the companionship is enjoyable. Next best to the school trips, Akira likes Obon and New Year's, when he is given substantial spending money for magazines, sweets, Western or Japanese movies in Ajino or Kurashiki, or anything else that he would like.

Like her brother, Yuriko associates mostly with her own sex. In the company of other girls she is learning how to sew and knit, and she has already knitted a cardigan of white nylon. She reads fashion magazines and many other magazines designed for girls and women. Her parents have talked about giving her lessons in flower arranging, and Kotomi, who is famed for her skill in this art as well as in arranging marriages, has promised to give lessons soon to the girls' division of the Young People's Association. Yuriko has recently become intensely interested in her appearance, and uses much of her spending money for lipstick, powder, eye shadow, and other cosmetics that she tries secretly in the company of other girls. Her mother and grandmother know, of course, but they are understanding, and Yuriko is careful to remove all traces before joining her father and grandfather. Her mother also has cosmetics—cold cream, face powder, and lipstick—that she uses sparingly on special occasions, just a touch to make her feel dressed up but not bold. Yuriko is waiting eagerly to become sixteen so that she may have her first permanent wave.

Girls a little older than Yuriko practice Western dancing together. Yuriko likes the phonograph records they play and sings the popular songs that come from America as well as the Japanese songs. She feels a little too shy as yet to join in the dance lessons; after all, most of the girls who do dance are eighteen and older and Yuriko is not always a welcome guest when they dance. Some of Yuriko's friends, a little older than she, talk romantically about boys, but Yuriko has little to say on the subject. She has learned about relations between the sexes from the same sources as her brother, with the addition of a brief, practical, and unnecessary explanation from her mother just last year at the time of her first menstruation. Yuriko is well aware of the premium placed on chastity in her community. The rare girl in the *buraku* who makes even one mistake of this kind is almost certain to be found out. She is then known as damaged goods, and there are serious problems when it is time for her to marry. Yuriko expects to enter marriage as a virginal bride, and, until marriage, she is content with the company of other girls. Like her brother, she enjoys best of all the grand holiday seasons, when she has much spending money and can wear her beautiful Japanese clothes.

Any time that the relatives convene is a pleasurable occasion. Since Hajime is the head of a household established for some generations, his family stays at home and entertains visiting relatives on the great holidays. These are times for special foods, rice cakes made with special glutenous rice, the finest fish, many other traditional dishes, and fruit. Sometimes in recent years, when Hanako has been pressed for time, the rice cakes have been purchased, but everybody likes to help make them. Hajime and Akira pound the steaming boiled rice with a large wooden mallet in a wooden mortar. In between strokes Hanako deftly turns the sticky mass of rice so that all grains will be pounded evenly. Yuriko and grandmother shape the pounded dough into cakes and dust them with a thin coating of wheat flour. Three especially large cakes, graduated in size and piled to form a tier, must be made at New Year's and placed in the alcove of the reception room as an offering to the gods. When finally removed days later, they are hard and dry on the outside but still delicious when toasted over the charcoal brazier.

Funerals are times of mixed joy and sadness. Commemorative services for the dead hold more joy than sadness, for most of the pain has been put behind. It is good to see the relatives, and there are many special foods even if fish is for a time prohibited according to Buddhist custom. The women must work hard to feed and care for the guests, but they do so willingly and the relatives help. The relatives bring gifts, especially for the children, and Hajime and Hanako are careful to see that the relatives leave laden with return gifts. For the small children even a funeral is fun—"Grandchildren's New Year's"—a wholly pleasurable time of good food and play with other children.

One other regular activity of the family, the hot bath, gives everyone pleasure. Baths are prepared twice weekly, and the family enters fairly much in the order of seniority. Depending upon the nature of the unfinished work at hand, grandmother and Hanako alternate in bathing last. Makoto still often bathes with his father, and sometimes with grandfather or his mother. Bathing is a combination of hygiene and pleasure. Before entering the tub the bather washes himself with soap, using water dipped from the tub with small bowls. He then steps into the tub, crouching in the water immersed to the neck for as long as the demands of courtesy for others will allow. The water is very hot, relaxing at all times, and particularly comforting in winter. Even in the warmest weather no one ordinarily dreams of taking a cold or cool bath. Until three years earlier the households of Hajime and his cousin Takashi had bathed together, alternating in preparing the tubs. During the heavy fishing season, when hot baths are taken more frequently, the same water was formerly used twice. These were both practices of thrift. It is expensive to heat the water, and filling the tub with buckets of water from the well is arduous work. Piped water and increased incomes have made these forms of thrift unnecessary and have brought others in their place. Bathing time is now often earlier than formerly, sometimes in the afternoon. When baths are finished, the hot bath water is used in the washing machine, thereby saving both money and labor on the part of Hanako and grandmother.

Worship

Hajime and his family are members of the Shingon sect of Buddhism, which has been the Buddhist religion of the community since its founding centuries earlier. Most of formal Shingon theology is unknown to them. They understand that they will all become Buddhas when they die; that their deceased ancestors must be given respect and attention; and that the ancestors should not be disgraced by improper behavior on the part of their living descendants. Some people maintain that ancestral spirits will cause harm if they are not cared for, but these are mostly the grandfathers and grandmothers. The closest Shingon temple is a mile from Takashima, and people of Takashima regard it as their own. With the exception of grandmother, Hajime's family rarely visits the temple, although they make annual contributions of money for its upkeep. Token attention is given by the family to the anniversary of Buddha's birth and to the annual Shingon festival commemorating its founder. Grandmother then visits the temple and makes an offering, but the rest of the family continues its ordinary activities.

For the most part Buddhism means that funerals and memorial services for the dead will be observed by traditional rites. These matters are in the province of the specialist, the local priest, who conducts rites in the homes of the deceased and at the graveyard. A funeral, which includes a procession with over twenty offices held by nearly forty persons who must carry paraphernalia and perform acts with symbolic significance, is much too complex an undertaking for the family to conduct or even understand. When Hajime's grandfather and grandmother died, it had been necessary to confer at length with the priest, to prepare in advance a list of the names and offices of the members of the funeral procession, and to hold what was in effect a rehearsal. The simpler memorial services that follow the funerals are held at fixed periods that lengthen as time passes and traditionally continue until the fiftieth anniversary of death.

The religion of everyday life of Hajime's family is not Shingon Buddhism but a mixture, predominantly Shinto, of beliefs and practices of many sources. Buddhist supernatural beings, other than The Buddha, tend to merge indistinguishably with Shinto gods and with other supernatural beings tracing their histories to ancient popular Chinese beliefs. Distinction of the gods according to their religious tradition is not a matter of importance. All the gods are beings of much the same order that have specialized provinces related to fishing, farming, the cure of disease, successful childbirth, and other human problems and endeavors. One should make offerings to them, fete them on many traditional occasions throughout the year, and he may ask their aid when it is needed.

The number of the gods known to Hajime's family and their neighbors is great, and conceptions of their attributes vary greatly. Most prominent among them is Kojinsama, the *buraku* tutelary god whose small shrine stands at the peak of the hill behind the dwellings. Kojinsama has powers over almost anything relating to the welfare of the community, but he is called upon most frequently when there is illness. Custom calls for two annual festivals in his honor, in spring and autumn, and other less important ceremonial visits to his shrine. Other gods of importance are associated with the dwelling, the God of the Kitchen and a generalized household god called Toshigamisama. Fishermen may regard as important Ebisusama, a god of good fortune, as well as Funadamasama, the God of the Boat.

According to grandfather and grandmother, the ceremonial calendar is very lengthy, with ceremonies marking the beginning and end of the agricultural and fishing seasons, many other lesser turnings of the seasons, and a host of other events. In the eyes of their juniors in the family, there are two important ceremonial occasions: Obon, when the ancestral spirits return in the late summer, and a long period at New Year's when little work is done. These are primarily holidays rather than holy days, although ritual is always observed. Some festivals that continue to be observed are wholly secular events for the children. There is Children's Day, a national holiday that combines the former Boys' Day and Girls' Day. There is also Tanabata, when the children write little poems, names, or wishes on strips of colored paper and attach them to bamboo branches.

In Hajime's household and in all others of the *buraku,* many of the events of the traditional ceremonial calendar today pass unobserved or receive only token attention. Even the festivals for the tutelary god are dying. Most people continue their usual work at such times and visitors to the shrine are principally grandmothers and their small grandchildren. The approach to Kojinsama's shrine is the only path in the community in which wild grasses grow.

A decline in faith coupled with loss of the necessary personnel have denied to Akira one of the privileges of young manhood. The ancient ceremony initiating youths into the Young Men's Association, which formed part of the Autumn Festival of the tutelary god, is no longer conducted. Held annually or biennially for young men turned sixteen, the rite celebrated their maturity with a feast in which they and all other unmarried young men of the community participated. It was a time when the young men buried their enmities with other youths and when all were allowed and expected to get drunk. Its climax was a procession of the drunken youths, in costume, carrying a heavy litter on which one of their number sat behind curtains beating a drum and impersonating the tutelary god. Scarcity of young men, lack of interest, and disapproval of drinking among the young recently put an end to this once popular event. Community dancing at Obon, once one of the greatest events of the year, had died out still earlier. For several years before the time that Obon dancing finally dwindled to an end, its participants had been mostly men and women of middle age, a few spry grandfathers and grandmothers, and small children. Young men and women watched the dancing sometimes, but usually said they felt too bashful to join in. Hajime and his family sometimes go to watch the dancing at Obon in larger communities nearby, where it serves as a tourist attraction and a commercial enterprise to stimulate sales for shops.

The decline of the gods is no less severe. However, the tiny shrines in houses, along paths between the houses, at the harbor, and in the forest are never wholly neglected. The aged and some of the more youthful tend them and try to preserve the old customs. At times of serious illness, the gods are still often remembered, after the doctor has been called. When critical protracted illness arises, the community unites to send a group of pilgrims to a prescribed series of shrines and temples in neighboring communities. Crises of this kind are now uncommon; conditions of health are good.

To most people the gods are still good, but they do not often come to mind. Other ways of doing things have replaced them. There is little conscious wish or will to change customs and beliefs. They have changed, as it were, of themselves, and many people regard themselves as being religious. Some things associated with the old gods have become bad, branded with the name of superstition. Grandparents may still consult the almanac to predict the future, tell of the terrible consequences of violating old taboos, and observe ancient Shinto rites of purification. For the middle-aged these are half-beliefs, and for the young they are generally little-known curiosities of the dim past. Some of the old beliefs have become amusing. Others are a little indelicate. Still other beliefs and customs that are openly called superstitions remain nevertheless alive. Lucky days are selected for marriage ceremonies and other important events, and thought is given to the dangerous years of life, especially to the forty-second year of a man's life.

Religious affairs in Hajime's family are left principally in the hands of grandmother. When she dies they will be borne by Hanako. Grandmother makes daily offerings of a few grains of rice to the God of the Kitchen and to Toshiga-misama, and on festival occasions makes special offerings. She seldom needs to remove the old offerings for they are usually consumed overnight by mice, which family members regard as endearing nuisances and are reluctant to kill. Grandfather tends the ancestors when he remembers to do so, making devotions before the tablets in the altar that bear their posthumous names. When the occasion calls for it, he gives honor to the ancestors at their graves. At these times other adult members of the family often join him.

Grandmother's normal speaking voice is modest and small, but she is a resonant intoner of Buddhist sutras and often participates in commemorative ceremonies for even distant relatives in the *buraku*. Grandmother visits the shrine of the tutelary god as well as the Shingon temple. When Akira and Yuriko were small children, they often accompanied her, but now they find other things to do. Makoto often goes with her, but he is reluctant to leave home when the hours conflict with those of his favorite television programs. He no longer wants to attend the New Year's eve ceremony at Kojinsama's shrine that had been one of the great delights of grandfather's and father's childhood. On this occasion he may stay up late in the company of other children and a few chaperoning adults, who sit about a bonfire inside the shrine toasting rice cakes and talking drowsily until midnight or even dawn. Makoto and his playmates complain that the shrine gets too hot and that there is nothing interesting to do. Hanako sometimes accompanies grandmother to the shrine and the temple, but after Makoto's birth grandmother had to remind her to take him to Kojinsama for the introduction required by custom the fourth month after his birth.

Grandmother sometimes worries about the laxness of her family toward the gods. Hajime has not formally visited the community shrine for many years, perhaps not since before he left for the war. He has, however, helped to repair the shrine and to clear the grass from the path leading to it. Most of the men of the community, grandmother is aware, have never been active in shrine or temple attendance, as this activity is understood to be more suitable for women. But modern times are seeing the women also grow lax, and Akira and Yuriko do not seem to know even the names of many of the ceremonial events. To be sure, three families in the community had this year joined the new Sōka Gakkai religion, but that had surely been a mistake if there were any truth in the bad things that the newspapers and most people in the *buraku* had to say about this strange Buddhist religion that forces people into membership. The new converts had talked zealously with Hajime and Hanako about joining, but they had not attempted *shakubuku,* "subdue and conquer," the forced conversion in which sustained pressure to join is exerted by a group of converters. Such tactics were not suitable among old neighbors and kin.

A few families had gone too far in another direction. Calling in the strange, old-fashioned mountain priests to drive out bad spirits by blowing conch shells and building smoky fires was surely not the best way to cure diseases. The doctors and the new health insurance had fortunately nearly eliminated those practices.

Grandmother's family had been Shingon Buddhist for as long as anyone could remember and, like herself, its women had not been remiss in giving attention to Buddha, the ancestors, and the native gods of Japan. Grandmother had made the customary long trips to ask the benediction of Kannonsama each time her daughter-in-law became pregnant, and she had always brought back with her the long cloth, received with Kannonsama's blessing, that was to be wrapped around the abdomen. She, or grandfather, had always willingly participated in the communal pilgrimages at times of critical illness in the community. Just before Akira took his entrance examinations for high school, grandmother made a special trip to a shrine near Okayama City for a talisman promising success in the exams, but it was received with politeness and no interest. She did not make the trip when Yuriko took the examinations.

Grandmother had seen a good many gods wither from neglect and a few die out entirely. No one today gives attention to the God of the Toilet or the God of the Well, and some people seem never to have heard of them. The first of these gods had been a little amusing even when she was young. There are others, however, such as Ebisusama, Daikokusama, and Konjinsama, and, most important of all, Kojinsama, whose neglect today is a graver matter. Their own family toilet, moved a dozen years ago from its original position to a place nearer the house, is surely in an inauspicious direction and one offensive to Konjin. When Hanako's third child died, grandmother gave serious thought to the reasons for his death. The immediate cause was the disease called infantile paralysis, of course, but she wondered why this disease should have struck him. She had finally talked with grandfather about the matter and they had both wondered aloud, in the presence of Hajime and Hanako, if it would not be useful to call for the services of a geomancer to prevent any future calamities. Nothing had come from their suggestion.

Still other instances of neglect disturb grandmother, but these she rarely mentions and then only to her agemates. When work allows her to do so, Hanako does not hesitate to eat with Hajime during her menstrual periods, and Yuriko does not even seem to know of this and other menstrual taboos. More serious is the ignoring of taboos during childbirth. Hanako had hardly been isolated at all, and after Makoto's birth she had not even performed the rites of purification. Grandmother recalled how she herself, when she gave birth to Hajime, had broken the rules of isolation just a little by going to the well for water before the end of the full period of her pollution. Old Heibei, then the grandfather at the main house, had been there and upbraided her in the sharpest terms for polluting the well. Embarrassed and ashamed, she had been careful not to leave her own yard until the full thirty-three days had ended and the rites of purification had been performed. She had also been careful to give no offense to the Sun Goddess by her unclean presence. When she stepped outside into the sunlight, she made certain that her head was covered with a cloth, and saw to it that the washed clothing of her infant and herself were hung to dry in the shadows of the eaves of the house. Perhaps it was right, as daughter Shizu had often said, that these old customs were disappearing. None of the women had liked them, but failing to observe them nevertheless gave her an uncomfortable feeling. Failure to observe the rules of avoidance and isolation when someone died was the most disturbing of all. Life during the period of mourning now went on very much as usual after two or three days, and her own family had already stopped holding the commemorative ceremonies for her husband's parents even though the last death had been only eighteen years ago.

Grandmother can adjust to these things, but doing so makes her feel a little strange. And nothing prevents her from praying to the old gods for the welfare of her family. Others of her age do so, and even some of the middle-aged and younger, at least when troubles arise.

Beyond the Family Circle

Hajime and his family form a closely knit group that acts in important matters as a unit. Its finances are family finances, and affairs important to any one member are important to all. Hajime controls these matters in ways that benefit all rather than himself or any other individual. Home is a fortress of security and the source of sympathetic understanding and support. Sympathy also comes from sources outside the immediate family. The peripheral relatives inside and outside the *buraku* are people to whom one feels close, although they are not people from whom the family should seek aid of any important kind, particularly financial, unless there is the direst need.

Everyone in the *buraku* belongs to many circles, formal and informal, that go beyond the family and are important in the tasks and pleasures of life. There are informal groupings of friends with common interests that may or may not follow lines of kinship. The largest informal grouping is composed of all those bearing the surname of Matsui, who hold themselves aloof from the several families with the surname of Otsuka. These Otsuka outsiders, whose history in the community is shorter than that of the Matsuis, are regarded as newcomers. Once very poor, the Otsukas are still not economically favored, and they are not admitted to the inner circle. Above all, marriage of a Matsui to an Otsuka is something to be avoided. Relations between the groups are nevertheless cordial if not intimate, and the Otsukas have full representation in community affairs.

Prestige and power in the *buraku* follow lines of wealth conditioned by former circumstances of familial status. The engineer Takao, the lone professional man in the *buraku,* is an outsider and a rank newcomer whose work is in a nearby community. Takao had married a pretty Matsui daughter and, because it was convenient for his employment, had built a new house in Takashima. His social status is high, but he is active in *buraku* affairs only to the extent of meeting minimal civic and social obligations. Clearly by his own wish, he stands somewhat outside the community scheme of organization.

Highest of all in prestige stands Rice House, which has for many generations held wealth and power. Rice House owns two boats, many nets, much farmland including rice paddy, and a grand house with many rooms. Rice House is also said to have investments in business firms in Ajino. Masaichi, its household head, is sometimes addressed by fellow Matsuis as "Mr.," a form of address otherwise used only between Matsuis and Otsukas, and for outsiders. Reasons for formality go beyond wealth. Rice House is estranged in many ways from the rest of the community, including its closest kin. Even Hajime's household, which began as a branch of Rice House, feels no love for Masaichi and his family, but care is taken not to express these feelings to others. Masaichi is clever, competent, forceful, outspoken, and self-seeking—and therein lies the trouble. He is often contemptuous of the ways of thinking and acting of his neighbors, whom he once described within their hearing as having peasant mentalities. Masaichi is well aware that his fellows have no love for him, but he is beyond reproof. Sometimes he insults the whole community in devious ways. When the Community Association held its meetings to make plans for a new harbor, he had become visibly annoyed at the slow pace of progress and stopped attending the meetings. In his place for several months he had sent his household's grandmother, who sat in rigid silence avoiding the eyes of other members.

Masaichi is not an outcast. He is merely disliked and avoided because of personal traits, and some measure of the dislike and avoidance is extended to all other members of his household. He is nevertheless a Matsui and a community member—and he is more than this. Masaichi is also a man thoroughly capable of dealing efficiently with the world outside the *buraku*. He is elected to office term after term as the *buraku* representative in affairs that involve the city administration, and he serves faithfully and well. With Masaichi in office, there is no fear of being represented by an "approver" who, seeking peace and goodwill at any price, follows the crowd. Approvers, as everyone knows, are all too numerous among the *buraku* household heads.

Other kinds of community problems are handled more informally without public airing. Crimes of any consequence are extremely rare. To be sure, various household heads have had trouble with income tax officials, who claim they have underdeclared their earnings. Tax evasion is not a matter of moral import. Every household underdeclares its income as much as it feels it dares. Those in trouble dared too much. In any case, the tax office understands these problems, and a compromise is reached soon enough. There are, however, certain small offenses that threaten the whole community. Isao's grandmother, otherwise a worthy and likeable woman, is a kleptomaniac who steals almost anything left unattended outside the dwellings and yards. Two young men are thought to be petty thieves. On two occasions houses were pilfered of money while their occupants were away. Circumstantial evidence pointed clearly to the two young men as the culprits; but the amount of money was small and no action was taken against them except to spread word quietly of their probable guilt.

A common solution for problems of this kind is to take safeguards against their recurrence. The few things, such as nightsoil buckets forgotten in the fields, that Isao's grandmother is now able to steal will in any case usually be returned by some member of her family with a brief, embarrassed apology. Relatives and neighbors can watch over house and household possessions when it is necessary for a family to leave the community. Problems such as these should not be referred to the police.

Among the formally organized *buraku* groups, the Community Association holds first importance. Every family belongs. Regular meetings are held monthly and special meetings are called to deal with unusual events. Hajime, as head of his household, usually goes as the family representative. He is reluctant to hold office in the association but has been elected twice, once as treasurer and later as head, and consented to serve out of a feeling of civic obligation. The community must do many things in unison, maintain the paths, the shrine of the tutelary god, the harbor, the community hall, and the communal drying racks for nets. Then there are the *buraku* festivals to plan and conduct, a matter which becomes more difficult each year. Many families have already expressed themselves in favor of observing the festivals in their individual homes rather than jointly.

Disputes over property lines and similar matters that rise occasionally can be handled judiciously at these meetings without the embarrassment and expense of recourse to law. Through the association, action can be taken by the *buraku* as a whole for damages incurred by outside parties. Last year countless meetings were held to prepare for submission to court a suit of damages—the first legal action of redress in *buraku* history—that asked compensation from the prefectural government for damages incurred to the community water supply. After the sea channel had been filled with soil and sand from the bottom of the sea, the people noticed that their wells produced somewhat salty water. This misfortune was explained by engineer Takao as the result of the pressure of the weight of the dredged soil and sand.

Hajime's family also belongs to the *buraku* Funeral Association, which assists bereaved families. Membership and faithful participation by one mature person, male or female, from each family is keenly felt to be a humanitarian obligation. Members of the Funeral Association notify relatives of the deceased, in person if possible; help to arrange the funeral; take care of all cooking and housework for the stricken family for several days; and help in many other ways to lighten the tasks of the bereaved and give them comfort. In addition, the association participates in funeral rites and later memorial services.

Young men belong to the *buraku* Fire Association, which holds regular meetings to give instruction and practice in firefighting techniques and springs into action whenever a fire occurs. Hajime is now the representative for his family. Akira will replace him when he is eighteen or twenty. Young unmarried men and women of age sixteen and above belong to the *buraku* branch of the Young People's Association. Once strong, this association now consists principally of girls. Even they seem to have lost interest in association activities.

The tottering Young People's Association is one of the many that have ties with outside communities. Some of the associations most important to Takashima people are organized on community levels larger than the *buraku* and their meetings are held in neighboring communities. Hajime's family belongs to the Fishermen's Cooperative and the Farmers' Cooperative, which has a women's division and a youths' division, both poorly developed because the Kojima area is one of mixed occupations. Both the fishermen's and farmers' associations are national organizations strongly encouraged by the Japanese government. Hajime faithfully attends and sometimes holds office in the Fishermen's Cooperative. As the principal farmer, Hanako attends meetings of the Farmers' Cooperative. These associations help to keep them informed of market conditions and new techniques of farming and fishing. Membership gives them many other privileges that are economically important. The cooperatives are the normal medium through which machinery, tools, and other fishing and farming equipment and supplies are obtained, and through which fish and farm crops are sold. The cooperatives are also the primary institutions of finance. Members maintain interest-bearing savings accounts in the cooperatives, borrow money from them at low rates of interest for use in connection with farming and fishing, and through the cooperatives obtain various types of governmentally-subsidized insurance against loss or damage to crops, livestock, and equipment. In addition, the Farmers' Cooperative sponsors many lectures of general interest to men and women. Hanako enjoys the visiting lecturers coming from the prefectural government who talk about diet, health, and other matters that are not directly connected with agriculture. The family may also go to the cooperative's stores to buy at reduced prices items of clothing, some foods, and other general merchandise.

The Parent-Teachers' Association gets Hanako's unfailing attendance. Grandmother also usually attends, as do even childless women of the community, for the P.T.A. is in many ways the successor to a more generalized women's society that had been important before World War II. Through the P.T.A. the women sometimes hear lectures on a wide variety of subjects including illustrated lectures on birth control. Men who attend the regular meetings of the P.T.A. are most commonly the few business and professional men included among the parents. Male heads of fishing and farming households like those of Takashima are not often present. Almost everyone attends when the school holds its annual sports meeting in the spring.

Representation by Takashima residents in other formal associations that draw memberships from many *buraku* is scattered. Hajime has long been a member of the District Crime Prevention Association. Crimes have been few and meetings in recent years have been mostly discussions, without ensuing action, of problems of juvenile delinquency in populous Ajino. A few of Akira's and Yuriko's friends from farm families belong to girls' and boys' 4-H Clubs. People who own rice land belong to the Irrigation Association, and Kotomi belongs to a women's society called the Cosmos Club that does water color painting and flower arranging.

Contacts with the outer world are increasingly frequent. In addition to participation in associations, Hajime, Hanako, and the children have many occasions to leave Takashima for shopping and recreation. Hajime and his family consider it a civic duty to participate in city, prefectural, and national elections, about which they are informed by the daily newspaper, radio, television, and campaigning sound trucks.

The Future

What the marital and occupational future holds for Akira is uncertain. Akira himself is very certain that he does not want to be a fisherman or farmer, and he harbors secret hopes of going to Tokyo, or at least to Osaka, when he has finished high school. College is beyond his horizons. Attending college requires money, and the fearful entrance exams for the good colleges eliminate most applicants. In Tokyo or Osaka he can receive technical training on the job in the schools of the great industrial corporations that are eager to engage young men like himself. His parents suggest that he might take employment in the new industrial plants of Kojima or neighboring Kurashiki. Akira is silent. What can these provincial cities offer to compare with the wonders of Tokyo, the largest city in the world, that he sees so often on television? Other young men who have taken jobs there have also made it clear, when they return to their old homes at Obon or New Year's, that Tokyo is a fabulously desirable place. But Akira is peaceful and says nothing about these dreams, even when grandfather in his impractical way talks of his becoming a fisherman and the head of the household.

Yuriko dreams less and sees the future more clearly. She plans to finish high school and take employment in one of the Kojima factories that make uniforms for schoolchildren, living with her parents and commuting to work. Employment in the factories, everyone agrees, is no longer a trial of ill-paid endurance. She will have money to spend for things for the family, such as the refrigerator they have long wanted. It will be only fair to help in this way, as her parents will be put to extremely heavy expense on her account for clothing, household equipment, and feasting at the time of her marriage. It is only fair also that Akira should inherit all the household property, as he will care for his mother and father in their old age. Yuriko will receive her share of the property in the money spent at the time of her marriage. From her employment, she will also have money for herself, for smart clothing, and for such things as a hi-fi set like the one her friend Sachiko owns.

Only occasionally and in make-believe does Yuriko think of moving to Tokyo. Her own observations agree, a little sadly, with the report by a sociologist that she once read in a magazine for young people: it is the ambitious and, especially, the pretty girls who most commonly go to Tokyo. Just perhaps, she sometimes thinks, someone handsome and clever like Isamu at school will propose marriage and take her on a honeymoon trip around the world—but, more likely, her parents will find someone quite satisfactory for her to marry.

The future of grandfather and grandmother is the most certain of all. They will live out their lives on Takashima, free of worrisome responsibilities, which are now, quite properly, borne by their son and daughter-in-law. Even grandmother is not fully aware how worrisome these responsibilities have become.

It is Hajime whose future is least certain and most disturbing. He knows no skill but fishing. The fast encroaching industrial plants dump refuse into the waters, and for the past several years he has seen the less competent fishermen of his community turn to other occupations. The price of fish is high and, with the help of the household farmland, the family is able to live in greater comfort than in the past. Representing his family, Hajime holds a life insurance policy, a postal savings account, and shares and a savings account in the Fishermen's Cooperative; Hanako has shares and a savings account in the Farmers' Cooperative. Socialized medicine keeps costs for ordinary medical care at a low figure, and the Public Health Service provides inoculations and x-ray examinations without charge. Hajime knows that profitable fishing cannot last and the future is a source of nagging worry to him.

Hajime lacks both the capital and the experience to do what he would like to do—start a small shop, perhaps one selling electrical appliances. The simplest alternative is unpleasant to consider after a lifetime of self-employment. He may easily find employment as an unskilled laborer in one of the industrial plants. These are things he tries to avoid thinking about, yet they are constantly forced upon him. At the many meetings of the Community Association of the past five years, grave misgivings about the future of Takashima fishing and farming have been voiced over and over again. No one worries about gaining a livelihood. Life grows more comfortable each year. The problem is to find a suitable way to meet the changing times. The life of a fisherman is not easy, but it holds its own attractions and gives a feeling of independence.

Then there is the growing problem of Akira's future, intimately tied with the problems that Hajime and Hanako face in their own lives. They hope that without pressure from them Akira will settle down at home, as Hajime did, and eventually become head of the household. It would be comforting to know that he would care for them in their old age and it would be good to have grandchildren in the house. But there are troubling doubts. Everyone knows that many grandparents in the cities do not live with their children and that some do not even want to do so. What is worse, opinion surveys published in newspapers and magazines made it clear that many young people do not want to live with parents and in-laws. It had taken three years to find a suitable bride for Eiichi, the son of neighbor Rikichi, and his only defect had been that he was the eldest son and heir in a farming family. Even a few of Hajime's own agemates express distaste for living out their old age as household grandparents. When her husband died, Hajime's sister Shizu had gone so far as to move to Osaka to support herself, alone at the age of forty-six. Always ahead of the pack and strong-willed, Shizu had done other unusual things. A zealous student in her school days, she had bullied her parents into allowing her to go to high school, paying the costs herself by working as a housemaid in a home in Ajino. Shizu had departed even further from convention by treating the outcasts of Hama *buraku* as seeming equals. She maintained an open friendship with one of the Hama women, a friendship that had been established when the two women attended primary school together, and even served tea to this woman in her home. Shizu had learned that many conventions could be broken with impunity, if one were firm and open in doing so and otherwise enjoyed a good reputation. As the female leader and intellectual of the *buraku,* she commanded respect, and even the head of Rice House deferred to her.

Explaining her plan to move to Osaka, Shizu had said firmly she would be no burden to her daughter and son-in-law, with whom she was on the warmest terms. Her remarks had made Hajime uncomfortable. He was, he knew, one of the "feudally-minded" people of whom the outspoken Shizu often referred with contempt. It had in no way been a consolation to hear that Shizu, at her age, could find employment only in a menial position.

Until the time that a bride was finally found for Eiichi, no word had passed between Hajime and Hanako about these matters, although she was aware of her husband's problems and sentiments. Grandfather had brought out the whole set of worries for family discussion. Complaining about the bride famine and the lack of seriousness of modern girls who seemed to have no filial piety, he had added that they would probably have the same problem in finding a bride for Akira. Speaking up without thinking of the consequences of her words, Hanako had said that it would probably depend on Akira. Hajime said nothing, which she interpreted to mean that he would abide by their son's wishes and that he too thought this the best course for all concerned, the one most suited to the changing times.

3

An Urban Family

Introduction

JIRO AND AKI MATSUI and their three-year-old daughter Emi live in an
apartment in Nerima Ward of Tokyo, where they have lived for three
years. Jiro, 32, is employed in the Tokyo offices of Asahi Industries, a
manufacturer of electrical appliances with factories and home offices in Osaka,
one of the largest concerns of its kind in the nation. Jiro works as legal advisor
in the legal department where his position holds precedence over several other
similarly trained men. His complaints are few, and he often congratulates himself
upon his good fortune. His salary is good, adequate to maintain his family and
himself in modest comfort and to keep him immaculately dressed in neat, dark
suits, in which he takes considerable pride.

Jiro's life is usually interesting and rewarding, and on the rare occasion
that he feels discontent, he takes comfort in reflecting upon what his life might
have been. Jiro is a modern citizen of Tokyo on an upward social and economic
path. The streets, trains, subways, and office buildings of Tokyo hold many men
like him, carefully groomed, educated "salary-men" whose prospects for the future are hopeful. Jiro makes efforts to be like the others, and he is generally successful. At home he sometimes slips into the ways of speech of Okayama or Osaka,
but the preferred speech of Tokyo with a trace of outside influences has become
natural to him. The southerly accent in his speech does no harm. He is employed
by an Osaka firm, and similar accents are plentiful among his associates and elsewhere in the city.

Aki, age 31, is the daughter of one of the many officials of Japan Enterprises, a concern affiliated with Asahi Industries. Born and raised in the Osaka
area and married to Jiro for four years, she has taught him a great deal in that
time. He has usually been a willing pupil, if sometimes puzzled and slow to understand. Aki is careful not to push or seem bossy, to put her instruction in the
form of suggestions and guidance. The things she teaches must be taught, but she

has both respect and affection for her husband. A college graduate, Aki speaks English and takes an interest in national and international affairs. She dresses well and is carefully groomed, as befits her station as the daughter of a substantial family and the wife of a promising man. Aki has many plans for the future of which her husband is not yet completely aware, although she has not really kept them secret.

Husband

VILLAGE LIFE   When Jiro was born his parents were none too pleased at the addition of another child to an already sizeable family. There was talk for a while of his adoption by his father's sister Shizu and her husband, who had a daughter but no son and little apparent prospect of having additional children. This idea was abandoned by Jiro's parents soon after his birth, to the disappointment of Shizu, who continued to take an interest in her nephew as an "almost" son. As the baby of the family Jiro received lavish attention from his sisters and, until her death in his third year of life, from his aged grandmother. There was little money and the food was coarse, but these were things of which Jiro was oblivious. His early childhood was one of indulgence by his elders and play with agemates. As the youngest child, Jiro was the possessor of an unusually great supply of toys, many of them originally purchased for his elder siblings and others purchased for him by his parents and Aunt Shizu. There were bouncing balls, tops, marbles, kites, swords, games, and even a tricycle purchased by Aunt Shizu the year her husband had such phenomenal success in mackerel fishing. Always sunny and compliant, Jiro was a joy to his mother and loved by everyone. Women relatives and neighbors often remarked upon his quickness and cleverness, and predicted that he would grow up to be a handsome man, leaving unspoken the implication that he would be nicer looking than his older brother, Hajime. For his own part Hajime looked upon Jiro with affection and tolerance. As Jiro grew older, Hajime sometimes played the role of helpful elder brother to him, but twelve years of age separated them and gave them different interests.

When Jiro began school he was quickly recognized as the prize student of his class, which at first pleased but did not especially impress his parents. By the nature of things some children and adults were clever and others were not. Jiro's mother had also been a prize student, but this accomplishment had not discernibly affected the course of her life. As the years passed, honors at school were heaped upon Jiro and, basking in his fame, he made serious efforts to enhance it. The principal of his school was reported to have called him a genius and to have said that he was an exceptional student for the *buraku* of Takashima, whose children often did not take school very seriously and generally excelled only in school athletics.

Setting his course as a student, Jiro also excelled in junior high school, and word of his triumphs reached home frequently. The principal, whose opinions were held in high regard, told Jiro's parents that he must go on to high school. Even though their eldest son Hajime had completed only the six years of schooling that was compulsory at the time, Jiro's parents valued education. Additional schooling, they reasoned, would serve no useful purpose in Hajime's future life as a fisherman and, in any case, they lacked the money. The only high school within commuting distance was private, which meant that there were tuition fees as well as other expenses. Hajime, now twenty-seven, was a full-fledged fisherman, so that there was no special need for Jiro's services at home. The schools always declared a holiday during the heavy agricultural season, and if Jiro's help were needed at other times, he could always be kept at home to meet the emergency. Jiro would not in any case stay home when he grew up, and a high school education would put him at better advantage for finding employment and establishing himself in adult life. The worst years of poverty following the war had ended, and with a little care the family could afford additional education for him.

Sending Jiro to high school was, however, not merely a matter of making the decision to do so. The local high school was overcrowded and the entrance exams saw admission denied to most of the applicants. Disturbing rumors circulated that success in the examinations was not the key to admission. Only sons and daughters of the rich could enter, it was said, and the only certain way of getting a son or daughter into the school was to pay a bribe to the principal.

Once committed to the course of sending Jiro to high school, his parents grew increasingly uneasy as they waited to hear the results of the exams. Shizu, who had been the first and for some years the only *buraku* girl to finish high school and who seemed to know everything that went on in the outside world, had come to them with a tale of bribery that named names and carried a worrisome ring of truth. Jiro's father talked of visiting the principal to confer with him about their son, but Shizu had branded that course as useless and had suggested another. Have the head of Rice House go visit the principal, she had recommended. As a relative and the head of their founding house, he would feel obliged to go, and as a city councilman he would have authority. Jiro's parents sent word to the main house that they wished to make a formal call, and the business was soon concluded. Two days later the head of the main house informed them that they need have no fears; the principal had reported that Jiro stood third from the top in the entrance examinations.

Success in gaining admission to the high school added fuel to Jiro's scholarly aims. He spent much of his time reading books. These were not merely textbooks. He read widely, borrowing books from the school library and exchanging with other students such magazines and books as they could afford to buy. These opened to him vistas of worlds far removed from Takashima and from the life of his agemates in the *buraku*. Jiro did not forsake the company of *buraku* boys of his age. He participated in less generous measure than others in all the customary activities of boys. He played baseball, caught *mejiro* with bird lime, played cards secretly in imitation of the gamblers among the elders, and once in a great while swam naked from the beach at the rear of the island. Jiro also participated in the festivals and in the company of the other youths had become enthusiastically drunk and ingloriously sick on his initiation to adulthood the year he turned sixteen. Jiro stood alone but the estrangement was one of differing interests, not ill feeling. Long ago he had learned to avoid the boys and girls from Hama with whom he attended school. At home, he spent no time with Otsuka boys, which met the approval of his parents, but he had only one enemy among the Matsui boys. This was Hiroshi, two years his senior, who teased him about his great swollen brain, and who once had urged him to set aside his books in favor of a joint visit to the whorehouse in Ajino. Hiroshi's ill will toward him was not a matter that he took very seriously. Everyone knew that Hiroshi was lazy and care-free, an inconsequential boy who spent far too much time playing his guitar and singing popular songs.

Jiro had his own dream for the future, one that had few precedents in Ta-kashima history. Jiro knew of only one, a second son of Rice House. Of course, there was no money at home to send Jiro to college, but he would work his way through, perhaps win a scholarship. Aunt Shizu was the person to talk with. He left her house in low spirits. She had told him that the prospect of his winning one of the few scholarships was remote and that working one's way through col-lege was still very hard, especially for a boy from the remote country. What is more, she had said, you know how difficult the entrance exams to good universi-ties are.

Shizu did not stop there. She promptly visited Jiro's parents to discuss the possibility of his entering college. Jiro was ideally suited, she pointed out, and if only money to send him could be found, the whole problem of his future would be solved. Perhaps she and her husband could help. Jiro's father and mother en-tertained other plans, not as yet firmly set. There was the traditional place for a second son like Jiro, and for a son of the quality of Jiro a preferred place of this kind could be found. He would help with the family fishing until he reached the age of marriage, when he would become a *yōshi,* the husband of a girl whose family lacked a son to carry on the family line. As the officially adopted heir of his wife's family, he would later become head of the household and hold a posi-tion of honor. There was of course strong sentiment against this kind of mar-riage. According to an old saying, as long as a young man had even one pint of rice bran he should never marry as a *yōshi.* But everyone knew that the custom usually worked out well enough after the husband settled down to it. The idea of college was at first a little startling to Jiro's parents and to Hajime as well, but they did not reject it offhand. Shizu, whose imagination had no limits, rounded up a flood of information on the cost of attending universities in Osaka, Kyoto, and Tokyo. The amounts were hopelessly high.

Jiro did not give up. He talked with his parents about the possibility of working his way through college. Since there seemed to be no valid ground for arguing against this course except for the worries they would have about his wel-fare, Jiro was allowed to make plans to take the entrance examinations. With soaring thoughts, he considered Tokyo University, the undisputed king of them all, but caution and Aunt Shizu's warning that Tokyo University's exams were the worst in the nation led him to settle for another. Shizu gave him an appraisal of the country's universities, which he later found to be somewhat oversimplified but in general agreement with opinion prevailing throughout the nation. For his own future welfare, she had said, he should study at one of the great national universities. If this were impossible, he could settle for a poor second best by attending a private or prefectural university. If worse came to worse, he could attend a private college. Kyoto University was her choice. It was a fine national university, and the city of Kyoto was both nearer home than Tokyo and a much cheaper place in which to live.

AT THE UNIVERSITY   Jiro took the exams for admission to Kyoto University, and after nervous waiting received word that he had been accepted. Aunt Shizu, who had much free time, accompanied him to Kyoto to help him find employment and a place to live. One week's stay exhausted their funds and left them with no hope. No one wanted to employ an inexperienced boy part-time, at least at wages high enough to make university life possible. Things looked hopeless, but at this time Shizu's husband died. After the funeral Shizu promptly set out for Osaka to live an independent life, leaving her home and lands to the care of Rice House. In Takashima the best she could hope for, she said, was the barest existence from cultivating her small farm herself and, when she grew too old to farm, unpleasant reliance upon the beneficence of relatives. Moving away would also eliminate another lesser unpleasantness. As a widow, living alone and still hale and hearty, she would soon enough be the subject of amorous overtures from a few of the more irresponsible household heads. These were difficult matters to handle without incurring ill feeling, and there was always the danger of damaging gossip even when she was entirely blameless.

A few weeks after moving to Osaka Shizu wrote that she had found a job. She had specified in her conditions of employment, she wrote, that her nephew would live with her. Jiro could commute from Osaka to the university in Kyoto by electric train. After showing the letter to Jiro and observing his reactions, his parents were not long in deciding to let him go. With Shizu supervising his behavior and welfare, they could feel at ease, for Shizu was "strong" in everything and regarded Jiro as if he were her own son.

In a state of nervous excitement Jiro met his aunt at the crowded railroad station in Osaka and was taken to his new home, an old frame building that adjoined a brick business office and warehouse. Shizu's employment was as housekeeper in the boarding house of a small Osaka company wholesaling metal pipes for domestic and industrial use. Her employer and his father before him had engaged country women like Shizu before and had found them paragons of thrift, industry, and loyalty. Shizu's duties consisted of buying food, preparing and serving three meals daily for thirty young unmarried men, and washing the dishes afterwards. It was her responsibility to see that the men received palatable food at absolutely minimal cost. Her working hours were from six in the morning until about ten o'clock at night, with some periods of light work and brief rest in between. She could take two Sundays of the month for rest.

Shachō-san, "Mr. Company Head," was a little close with money, Shizu told Jiro, and she had to be very careful in her buying. Shachō-san had set the daily allowance for food for one person at a figure barely enough to buy a lunch at a cheap restaurant or a ticket to the cheapest movie. It was enough, Aunt said, if she were very careful in shopping, but Jiro would have to be prepared for whale meat and many other foods to which he was not accustomed, and no fruit whatever unless purchased with their own money. Meat, she said, would consist of much whale meat, occasional small servings of pork, and, rarely, scraps of chicken left over at the butcher's after the fowl had been dismembered for piece sale to richer customers. To Jiro, who was unaccustomed to meat, this seemed a luxury. The portions turned out to be minute, but Shizu's skillful serving of the meats in tiny strips and pieces placed atop a bowl of noodles or rice somehow made them appear substantial.

Kitchen equipment for Shizu's use consisted of a few pots, pans, and implements; three gas burners for cooking and heating water; a small cold-water sink; and a refrigerator for use in the heat of summer and for storing Shachō-san's beer. Food was served in a concrete-floored dining room, just large enough to accommodate three rough wooden tables with narrow benches. The boarders shared tiny bedrooms that were reached by a steep staircase from the dining room.

Shachō-san's office, a large room equipped with an oscillating electric fan for summer use and a gas heater for the winter, was separated from the boarding house by a narrow passage. It was also Shizu's duty to clean this room, which contained a huge desk, two sofas, several large overstuffed chairs, a table for serving refreshments to guests, and, prominently displayed, a bag of golf clubs and a bookcase containing elegantly bound books on Japanese folklore. When Shachō-san had guests, Shizu served them tea and confections especially kept for such occasions, and sometimes the beer that cooled in the refrigerator. Shachō-san maintained a car and a chauffeur, who also needed to be served tea but not beer.

Shizu's sleeping quarters, to be shared with Jiro, shocked him a little. Their room, at the head of the stairs, measured six by nine feet and had an added closet. It would do for studying, Aunt Shizu pointed out, because the boarding house was quiet in the evening, when the boarders usually went elsewhere and she herself was busy downstairs. Jiro adjusted quickly enough to the food and his new associates. The boarders liked him and seemed pleased to have a university student in their midst. The boarders all liked Aunt Shizu, too, although many of them treated her with what seemed to Jiro brusque casualness. Shachō-san was civil if not friendly, and he too seemed to take some pride in having a university student in the house.

There were, however, problems for both Shizu and Jiro. The company office and boarding house were on a busy thoroughfare where trucks and cars rumbled and sounded their horns until late at night, disturbing their sleep. When Shizu finished her work at ten o'clock she was tired and fit only for rest. She craved a bath every night, a luxury which the boarders could not afford and which she had not enjoyed on Takashima. Life, she said, was not possible otherwise. The public bath, two blocks away, closed at eleven. By the time Shizu reached it she found the water displeasingly murky from its heavy use in the preceding hours. Shizu had often complained about the thrifty cast-iron bathtub back at home in Takashima, calling it a cannibal pot, but it now seemed luxurious as compared with the congested public bath. Ever resourceful, she soon devised a way to bathe in the kitchen by heating the water on the largest gas ring and placing it in a large wooden tub intended for kitchen use. It was not a proper bathtub in which they could immerse to the neck, but it was clean, hot, convenient, and cheap. Shachō-san lived far away and need not know. When the bath was finished, Jiro could study at the kitchen table beneath the lone electric light.

Jiro and his aunt arose at the same time, for his travel to the university in Kyoto took well over an hour by subway, electric car, and on foot. Gulping breakfast and thrusting into his school bag a lunch consisting chiefly of rice, Jiro was off. For many months the trip was exciting, and he soon became adept at pushing his way through the crowds. University life was exciting, too, even if he lacked the money that many of the students spent so lavishly. The school uniform was a blessing that helped conceal his poverty, but school expenses seemed nevertheless high, especially because of the cost of daily commuting. His family sent what they could, and Shizu gave what she could. In all, it was enough, but barely enough.

For Jiro there could be none of the pleasures of the richer students, no hours of chatter to the sound of Western classical music or jazz in the pleasant surroundings of coffee houses, no occasional bottle of beer, no movies, and certainly no dates with girls. Some of the students were frighteningly sophisticated, speaking of Western art, music, and food with the familiarity of connoisseurs and sprinkling their conversation liberally with English and French expressions. Some had their own cars and apparently limitless money to spend, and these seemed to know much about bars and cabarets and women of the "water-trades," entertainers and bar hostesses. Jiro had no money for even a bowl of hot noodles, the cheapest item of fare at the restaurants patronized by students, but there were other students like him and he found the circumstances tolerable. Only one of the pleasures denied to him caused yearning. He eagerly read every article on skiing that came his way, spent hours standing in the book stores reading, free of charge, sports magazines that contained articles on the subject, and haunted sporting goods stores that carried skiing equipment.

Exams came and Jiro found that his crown for brilliant scholarship had vanished. The grades were solid but gave him no special distinction. He did not need Aunt Shizu to explain that he was no longer in the country. He was confronted with that knowledge daily, in countless ways besides his record at the university. It had been a little embarrassing at first to use the pronunciations and forms of speech customary at the university. They were not new to him; it was the matter of using them habitually that was new. At the boarding house he spoke his native Okayama dialect with Aunt Shizu, and from the boarders and casual contacts elsewhere he quickly learned the Osaka manner of speaking, which was more colorful but otherwise not very different from his native speech.

When the short summer vacation came, Jiro and Aunt Shizu were out of funds and there was no prospect of more from home. Shizu talked with Shachō-san about Jiro. The employees of the firm, she had noted, were nearly all young and several were no older than Jiro. Hard-working employees of any age were not easy to find because of competition from large firms that offered more. Middle-aged men were few and they all held positions of responsibility that required long experience. There were no old men. Retirement came at the age of fifty-five when the retiring employee received a lump sum equal to two years' earnings—and promptly sought some kind of employment elsewhere as a temporary employee at lower wages. These were matters of business frugality, she knew, as wages rose with years of service and numbers of dependents.

With the air of a paternal benefactor Shachō-san readily agreed to take on Jiro as a temporary employee during the summer and winter vacations. The work was principally manual labor connected with loading and unloading stocks. Jiro was also a useful errand boy, who could be relied upon more than others not to dawdle on the way and whose personal appearance was an asset to Shachō-san on such occasions. He was soon entrusted with important errands to other business firms and, after a time, to the bank with small amounts of money. At these times he was instructed by Shachō-san to wear a money belt tied about his waist to prevent theft by the skillful Osaka pickpockets. His fellow employees were friendly and protective, and with those near his own age there was often educative banter in racy Osaka speech. From his fellow workers Jiro learned that Shachō-san kept a *nigo-san,* a "Madam number two." This information was imparted with a tone of envious admiration and was followed by bantering speculation. If the boss got rid of his mistress, one boy ventured, perhaps he could pay them a better bonus. No, another said, if he had to spend all his time with his wife, his disposition would be so bad that they probably would not get any bonus at all. Shachō-san's wife, he said, was the original model of *deppa,* the bucktooth, whose teeth projected so that one could not bear to look at her twice.

The boarders seldom stayed in their rooms at night but instead sought more lively atmosphere wherever their interests took them—to pinball parlors, third-run movies, night baseball games, and, after paydays, sometimes to neighborhood bars and bawdy houses. No one urged or expected Jiro to join in these activities. His world was a different one.

Life for Jiro was not an unremitting cycle of work. His studies at the university took much time, but they consisted principally of memorizing, at which he was proficient. Among his professors Jiro had earned the reputation of being a reliable, sincere, and unusually courteous student. The swirl of extracurricular activities of other students passed him by for lack of both money and time to be in Kyoto. There was nevertheless always some free time that might be spent in the companionship of students as poor as himself, and occasionally there was a little spending money. He and his friends could roam the busy streets in the shopping and entertainment areas of Osaka, visit the free exhibits of art and photography in the department stores, and go sight-seeing. Jiro soon learned which areas of the bustling city to avoid. Once the lesson was costly. With friend Kiyomi he had wandered about in the Shinsaibashi shopping area, enjoying the brilliant neon lights, the crowds of people, and the displays in the shops. Jiro carried with him a thousand yen, all except fifty of which were for the purchase of books. His eye was struck by a shoe-shine stand in a side street near an area bright with the lights of pinball parlors and bars. Impulsively he decided to experience the pleasure of his first professional shoe shine, which should be well within the limits of his spending money. When the *mompei*-clad woman finished she looked up at him with an expression that seemed curiously apologetic and said, "One thousand yen, please." Three young men with long sideburns, tight Western suits, and shoes with sharply pointed toes appeared from nowhere and looked at him meaningfully. Jiro gave all his money, and Kiyomi also emptied his pockets. The men were members of the Kitama-gumi, one of the most powerful gangster organizations in the city, Kiyomi told him later. The walk home took an hour and a half.

The years of university life passed pleasantly enough. The family was increased by a mongrel dog, black and smooth-haired, that Jiro picked up as a newly weaned puppy in the train station in Osaka. Jiro had seen similar puppies and kittens at the station and in the streets, abandoned by owners reluctant to do away with them, but he had always passed them by. This small puppy, its head protruding from a hole in a cardboard box that bore a sign saying "Cute puppy. Won't someone care for it?" had struck a sudden chord of sentiment. Impulsively tucking the dog under his arm, he had taken it home. Aunt Shizu was pleased, and Shachō-san said that it was good to have a watchdog. They called him Kokuban, Blackboard, and he joined Shizu and Jiro in the kitchen.

The noises of traffic on the busy street before the boarding house had soon become familiar sounds that disturbed Jiro not at all. The food was poor and the winter sometimes unpleasant with no heat but a bed warmer, and there was never enough money to take Jiro home at New Year's or Obon even on the cheapest slow train. He accepted these conditions as a matter of course. Accustomed to unheated classrooms, he felt really uncomfortable only during the intense, breezeless heat of summer and in the dead of winter when he tried to study in the drafty kitchen. Aunt Shizu fared much worse than he. Torpid and weak in the oppressively humid summer, hands black with chilblains in the winter months, and red-eyed from exhaustion in all seasons, she finally admitted defeat. In November of Jiro's last year at the university, she told Shachō-san she was thinking of returning home to Takashima in the spring, when Jiro received his degree. Shachō-san raised her wages a little, installed a heater in her room, a water heater in the kitchen, promised her an extra-large bonus at the end of the year, and ordered a tailor to make for Jiro a fine suit of clothing fit for a budding lawyer. Under this load of indebtedness Shizu did not again bring up the possibility of leaving Shachō-san.

Jiro received his degree as a student of good but not distinguished standing, well liked by his professors. The degree rather than individual performance was, he knew, the important thing. He knew also that he was in a favored position for employment. The largest and best corporations, those that paid the highest salaries, provided the most ample fringe benefits, and offered the greatest possibilities for advancement, were within his reach. Campus gossip had told him long ago that the biggest and best firms limited their hiring to graduates of two Tokyo schools, Tokyo University and Hitotsubashi University, and his own Kyoto University. Graduates of lesser schools went to lesser companies. He stood a good chance for lifelong employment by a desirable if not the most desirable concern. His salary would be small at first, but would rise as a matter of course as he grew older and acquired a family. Once employed, the prospect of his ever being offered or accepting employment by another firm was small, as was the prospect of being discharged for indifferent or inadequate performance. With luck, he might rise to a position as a lesser official. His talents would probably be inadequate to take him farther, lacking as he was in social background and influential connections.

THE URBAN SALARY-MAN   During his final year at the university Jiro was interviewed for employment by several large business concerns. In January Asahi Industries offered him employment after a series of personal interviews and examination of his written personal history, which included extravagant endorsements by his professors. Asahi's scrutiny of his family background showed nothing worse than unexceptional rural poverty. His beginning monthly salary was to be more than twice that of Aunt Shizu, and he would receive the equivalent of nearly a half year's pay annually in bonuses paid in summer and at the end of the year. In addition, he could eat inexpensively at the company dining room and participate in many forms of recreation subsidized by his firm. He could say with pride that he was a salary-man employed by Asahi.

Shachō-san at the pipe company offered no objection to his continuing to live with Aunt Shizu; instead, Shachō-san seemed pleased, and sometimes on Saturday afternoons invited Jiro to join him in drinking a glass of beer in his office. Jiro now found his lodgings confining. As a young man turning twenty-three, he had tasted few of the pleasures of young male life and was eager to try them. Aunt Shizu herself suggested that it would be much better for him to live in the Asahi dormitory, and he quickly agreed. His new quarters, shared by a roommate of the same age, seemed to him luxurious. The large concrete dormitory had a dining room where he could eat if he pleased and a bath with plentiful hot water. Even the company food seemed delicious. To his great surprise, he heard from more sophisticated fellow employees that the food was bad.

Work went well and was far from difficult. The department head, Mr. Kodama, was autocratic, and strict seniority prevailed. A lifetime of following rules without demur found Jiro well prepared to accept the order of things, and he was soon regarded as a trustworthy member of the group. Work proceeded at a leisurely pace, with ample allowances of time for tea and rest. When a task of any importance was put before him, he won the approval of the department head by remaining to work after the customary quitting hour.

The leisure hours were unalloyed pleasure. Saturday afternoon and Sunday were completely free, and there were many other holidays during the year. These were times for the untasted joys. He participated in sports with fellow employees, and began setting money aside for a ski outfit. His eagerness led him to heights of thrift as the goal drew near, and he took to going without lunch. Within eighteen months he was completely equipped and on a ski train with companions from Asahi. The trip from Osaka was long, but by traveling on the cheapest trains, where they often had to stand, and staying in the cheapest lodges wedged in with companions, the cost was lowered. Jiro quickly learned to ski, and found the sport no less enjoyable than his imagination had made it.

Back in Osaka there were many pleasures—movies, *sumo* wrestling exhibitions, and outright masculine diversions of other kinds. He met girls employed by Asahi and through them and his male friends was introduced to still other girls. His first date was in the company of another couple, but he soon found it pleasant to date alone. He discovered the pleasures of coffee houses and spent long hours in them, in groups with other young men and girls, or dating alone. The coffee houses were especially good when funds were low or when he had a special date. The good coffee shops had "mood," a romantic atmosphere created by elaborate furnishings, soft lights, and music. He could sit with enjoyment for hours on a soft plush chair over a single tiny cup of coffee, talking, and sometimes only listening to the music. There were occasional special dates, too, for late-hour coffee shops with pullman seats and unusually dim lights. He learned where to find the *abekku,* the small inns catering to couples wanting "short rests" that abounded in the tortuous alleys of the entertainment areas, and visited a few from time to time. The rooms, he was amused to discover, often had a mirrored wall, discreetly covered with sliding panels of wood or opaque draw curtains within convenient reach from the bed for those who wished to open them.

There were also occasional drinking parties in male companionship that followed the weddings of department members or just arose of themselves on Saturday nights and during the New Year's season. After the bonus was paid in December, an expedition of expensive "ladder drinking" usually followed that took the group from bar to bar to final oblivion. The nights on the town sometimes took the group to places less savory than the most dimly lit of the coffee shops. When the group was in a "pink mood," they watched the performances of stripteasers and went to places where they enjoyed the companionship of bar hostesses, female Turkish bath attendants, or undisguisedly professional brothel girls. The bar hostesses were particularly pleasing company even if expensive. At a good bar, where the girls were pretty, the fees for their company and for the watered whiskey they drank could run to a staggering figure in just a short time. Of course, no one should take those girls seriously, but they did know how to make a man feel clever, masculine, and important. "Mr. Attorney" they called Jiro, and he was surprised and pleased to see how witty he was while in their company.

For Jiro these were enjoyable but wholly casual events. He had no serious romantic interests, and he would not be ready for marriage for several years. There were no excesses. These were prevented by both lack of money and personal inclination. It took a large part of Jiro's money to keep himself appropriately dressed. A suit of clothes cost a month's salary or even more, although with care it had a long life. As a proper salary-man Jiro also needed suitable accessories—expensive cufflinks, neckties, and a wristwatch—and he must have sparklingly clean shirts, changed daily without fail. Expenses were high but Jiro, with an eye to the future, unfailingly put aside a sum of money each month.

During his second year of employment Jiro returned to Takashima for the first time since leaving for the university. Aunt Shizu accompanied him at his expense, and it was a time of mixed emotions. It was wonderful to see his parents and all the other relatives, but life on Takashima seemed so much cruder than he had remembered. His reception by the more distant relatives and old playmates was stiff. Neither side had much to say. His old enemy Hiroshi briefly greeted him with evident embarrassment when they accidentally met in the path and hurried on. A painfully shy boy and a girl, both high school students, came to ask him questions about universities. Before the visit was over he was longing for Osaka. He returned to Takashima only once again before his marriage.

Back in Osaka, life went on as before. Jiro's reputation as a reliable employee grew. Mr. Kodama had several times commended him for fine performance, and in Jiro's twenty-sixth year, asked him to prepare for and take the examination for qualification as a patent lawyer. Accepting the request as a command, Jiro agreed with fluttering heart. Only one of twenty aspirants was successful in passing that examination, he knew, and he nervously began a course of study, alone at night, that made it necessary for him to forego most of his customary pleasures for ten months. Jiro realized that he had been honored, but the full extent of his special status was not clear to him until some weeks after his home study had begun. At the office party to see off the old year, a time when frank words often passed without later retaliation, one of his associates had referred to Mr. Kodama as Jiro's *oyakata*, his "father," and the others had laughed. Rather than seeming displeased, Mr. Kodama also laughed and, placing his arm around Jiro's shoulders, exchanged drinks with him. Now fully aware of the responsibility laid upon him, Jiro redoubled his efforts, putting aside even the pleasure of skiing.

When examination time came in September, Jiro was thin from exhaustion and nervous. The last week before the exam saw him studying nightly until two or three in the morning, when he fell asleep fully dressed. The examination went successfully and, to Jiro's surprise, Mr. Kodama told him to take two days off for rest. Upon his return to work some of his fellow employees seemed changed, a little more formal in their behavior toward him. Mr. Kodama clearly seemed to regard him as a protégé, and a few days later invited Jiro to lunch with him at the Osaka Grand Hotel, one of the finest hotels in the city. The business at hand was finally broached as they neared the end of their special Kobe beefsteaks and reached a conclusion over off-season melon and a demi-tasse. Would Jiro like to meet a young woman of marriageable age, well reared and attractive, who was a niece of one of the vice-directors of Japan Enterprises, and also a niece of Mr. Kodama? Jiro's first impression of Aki was that she was considerably less attractive physically than he had been led to imagine, but there was no doubting that she was well reared and mannerly. Later his impressions grew much more favorable. The wedding was finally set for October of the following year.

Wife

THE URBAN FAMILY LIFE   Aki Kodama was born the fourth child and third daughter of parents stemming on both sides from families with long lines of tradition in commerce. None had known poverty, and some had been wealthy. The Kodama family home is in Nishinomiya City, in a neighborhood composed of similarly well-to-do families, most of whom derived their livelihood from employment in neighboring Osaka. The house is neither new nor a mansion, but it is eminently respectable. Its four sleeping rooms are of Japanese style, as is a large reception room adorned with valuable antique scrolls and flower vases that are changed with the season and the type of flowers on display. Most of the rest of the house leans toward Western style. There is a Western room, furnished long ago, that is crowded with a small grand piano and heavy furniture copied after models of a bygone day. The dining room was furnished recently with a Western table and chairs, and the kitchen is equipped with a refrigerator, a gas stove and a water heater, and many small electric appliances. The Japanese bathroom, large and luxurious, has a new sunken tub of pale aquamarine tile, and a terrazzo floor inset with polished stones of pastel tints. Added to these rooms are a storage room, an attic, a garage for the family sedan, and a small sleeping room for the maid. The garden, arranged with the guidance of a landscape artist, follows Japanese tradition and is both cooling and soothing to look at in the summer months. Aki's parents have sometimes talked of building a new house in more modern style but both know this will never come about. The old house is sound, comfortable, and certainly no discredit to them, and a new one of proper sort would be prohibitively expensive.

Aki's upbringing had been careful and wholly urban. Denied none of the privileges of girls of her class, she received thorough training in all the social graces. Some of the Kodama relatives were admittedly a little coarse, in the Osaka merchant tradition, and unabashedly concerned themselves with turning a profit. A little sensitive about this matter Aki's parents had raised their children in ways that seemed more genteel. They themselves, however, did not hesitate to use Osaka speech when the occasion demanded. Although secretly deplored, such expressions as the Osaka greeting "Are you making any money?" often passed Mr. Kodama's lips in addressing relatives and business associates. Favored rather than rich, the Kodamas depended for their position in part upon the influence of richer relatives.

Mr. Kodama holds a position of some stature as a company official, but his career had been a little disappointing to his father, who until his death a few years earlier had held higher eminence in the same concern. A college graduate at a time when they were few, and well connected through influential relatives, Mr. Kodama has gone less far than others so favored. His college training at Tokyo University had bred in him a disdain for trade. Reluctant to plunge whole heartedly into the commercial world, he valued the cultivation of manners and esthetics above other affairs. These were tendencies readily evident to the shrewd eyes that had watched him. Valuing kinship, their owners were also keenly aware of the need for the right man in the right place. There was certainly a place for him, however, and one with moderate authority.

Mr. Kodama's salary is good, and he is well enough placed with the corporation hierarchy to qualify for liberal use of an expense account in entertaining guests important to the company's affairs to whom his tastes and personality are suited. His wife's family is quite as influential as his own. Although a little less affluent than many of their kind, the Kodamas hold an honored position. In part from necessity and in part because this virtue is also in the commercial tradition, the Kodamas practice some forms of thrift and have taught them to their children. All of the Kodama daughters were taught to cook, and all took pleasure in doing so, although the bulk of the work rested always upon the family maid of all work.

CHILDHOOD AND COLLEGE   Aki learned to play the piano, to arrange flowers, and to conduct herself with gracious propriety in the presence of elders. Her tastes and training spanned both East and West. Western art and classical music were familiar to her from early childhood, and the family diet customarily included various Western dishes. She had been an enthusiastic member of the Girl Scouts and an equally enthusiastic participant in school excursions. With parents or other relatives she had visited many parts of the nation by the time she finished college. Without becoming a Christian or even considering the possibility, Aki had attended a Christian mission college for girls in nearby Kobe together with hundreds of girls like herself, for whom such schools provided a properly refined atmosphere and good training in the prestigeful English language. The family religion was Shin sect Buddhism, taken very lightly.

Aki's record as a student was good. She had belonged to the English-speaking Society and the Poetry Club but had never held office in either. For a time in her teens she had secretly written sad poetry, and she had rebelled against her given name, saying that it was old-fashioned. These had been momentary fancies. Along with other girls she had experimented, in seclusion, with strange hair styles and cosmetics, talked of boys and romances, practiced Western dancing a little and had even talked for a time of becoming an airline hostess. In public her appearance and behavior were exemplary.

In the private high school for girls that she had attended, Aki had daringly followed the lead of other girls and entered an "s"-kankei relationship with Takae, a boarding student from Hiroshima, two years her senior in age and school class. The girls had pledged to act eternally as faithful sisters, and this bond allowed them to depend upon each other and to share their most secret joys and sorrows. Their pledge had to be kept secret from the teachers, who looked upon the "s"-kankei as having undesirable sexual implications, but to all the other girls the secret was open. Some girls said that the "s" came from the English word "sex"; a few others thought it came from the word "sister." When the two girls were alone, Aki called her friend "elder sister," and, following convention, she had sent a few confidential messages to her so addressed. Aki, in turn, was addressed by her given name. Within a few months the relationship had fallen apart from lack of substance. There had been so few secrets, and no crises or emotional needs arose.

Aki emerged from college a young lady both modest and modern, refined in speech, dress, walk, and gesture. She had no romances and only rarely had dates. Her mother had often remarked to her husband and women kinfolk what an easy child Aki was—gentle, obedient, and polite. In later life, as Aki finished college, her mother sometimes felt moments of regret that her youngest daughter showed so little individuality. Her sisters and her brother had been more troublesome, but they had also been more interesting.

PREPARING FOR MARRIAGE   When Aki finished college at twenty-two, she talked a little of taking employment somewhere, but soon gave up the idea in deference to the mild opposition of her parents. She would soon marry, they thought, and there were few opportunities for suitable employment for a girl who had finished college with a degree in sociology. Aki had seen her brother and her three sisters marry and marry well. The girls were all pretty and their marriages, compromises between tradition and personal preferences, had not been difficult to arrange. Through the multiple skeins of kinship and personal connections, prospective bridegrooms for Aki were proposed and their qualifications discussed by her parents. Two introductions were arranged during the first year after her graduation from college, and Aki surprised her parents by politely but flatly expressing disinterest in both young men. Even more surprising was the lack of interest in Aki on the part of various prospective bridegrooms of proper station. A few, they were given to believe, did not want to marry a college graduate; such girls were too independent and bossy. Most others had no objection to a college education but demurred on other unstated grounds.

It became increasingly clear that arranging a suitable marriage for Aki was not an easy matter. Additional young men were reviewed but yielded only a few acceptable candidates that expressed interest. By the time Aki reached the age of twenty-six she had quickly put an end to four tentative overtures and was left with no prospects in sight. Aki herself expressed a desire to marry but seemed both unhurried and unworried. Her life revolved about the members of her family and diminishing relations with girlhood friends.

Much of Aki's time was spent with her sister-in-law and her two children. Brother Hisashi, thirty-eight, and his wife and children shared her parents' home and would expectably become its owners eventually. Hisashi was a rising employee of Asahi Industries, and the nature of his work was special. Expansive, persuasive, and convivial, Hisashi was the talented customer's man who spent many nights of the month entertaining important Japanese and foreign representatives of concerns with which Asahi had business relations. Most of the visiting representatives liked and expected an expensive fling, and for this Hisashi was well suited by temperament and physical capabilities. Drink and rich food did not befuddle him and left their mark only in a slowly expanding waistline and eyes that were beginning to look a little unwholesome. Hotels, steakhouses, theaters, cabarets, night clubs, the *geisha* quarters of Kyoto, elegant brothels, and Turkish baths were his frequent haunts, at which the expenses for an evening sometimes exceeded his monthly salary. Hisashi's friends in the water trades numbered in the hundreds, and as a special representative of Asahi Industries he was always warmly welcomed by them.

Hisashi's special talent lay in judging the tastes of his guests and he seldom erred. For the minority who disliked lavish foods and gamy entertainment, he was a considerate host who could talk a little on almost any subject and listen attentively. He was quite as much at home in the constrained elegance of inns such as Nishinomiya's Harihan, where guests were limited to those appropriately introduced, as he was in the late hour company of the *geisha* of Gion or their modern counterparts in cabarets and nightclubs. Hisashi's work exacted a toll from his wife, who sometimes saw little of him for days at a time except his sleeping figure, insensible to the early morning activities of the household. These trying conditions would come to an end in a few years, she was told, as Hisashi was scheduled for promotion to the position of executive director of sales, in which capacity he would seldom need to spend the nights in wooing customers. In the meantime, she had her children, and Aki was always available for adult companionship.

To Aki's parents the issue of her marriage became urgent. She must marry soon or expect a lifetime of spinsterhood. Appraising her assets candidly, they were forced to acknowledge that Aki was not pretty. The prospective husbands she had refused to consider had had little to recommend them along these lines, to be sure, but masculine beauty had seemed to them a trivial matter. The sweetness of Aki's personality had disguised for them her lack of beauty, but her plainness was probably very apparent to those who did not know her well. Perhaps there were other considerations. The family had an esteemed social position but no great wealth or authority that might serve to override other shortcomings. And the girl herself was no help. Otherwise tractable, she could clearly speak her mind on the subject of a husband for herself. There had been unmistakable finality in her refusals.

The procedure now was to try at a lower level, to search for a young man of promise who might be deficient in social beginnings. There was nothing new in this action; it was honored by centuries of usage. Everyone knew that some of the most prominent men in the nation including the most highly paid business executive of the present day had sprung from very lowly backgrounds. When the possibility of marriage to Jiro was brought up, Aki was a virginal but undeniably full twenty-seven. She expressed willingness to meet him and did not hesitate afterwards to say that she liked what she had seen.

Regarding themselves as progressive young moderns, Aki and Jiro were reluctant to proceed with a marriage that was arranged in a wholly traditional way. They wanted to be sure themselves of their willingness to marry, and this attitude was understandable to everyone concerned. Jiro and Aki began a series of engagements, conducted with the utmost propriety. There were movies at the finest theaters, visits to art exhibits, and, with tickets provided by Aki's parents, sometimes concerts and other musical performances. Jiro talked of skiing and was delighted to know that Aki also could ski. In the chaperoning company of other young men and women, they made a trip to a ski resort in the Japanese Alps. Jiro was no less pleased with Aki's ability to speak English, a language which he admired but was quick to admit that he could not speak despite years of studying it in school. Like many of his associates he could read the written language fairly well but had never mastered the difficult sounds of verbal English. In a few months questions and doubts vanished, and definite plans for the marriage were made. Jiro and Aki found themselves visiting the more decorous of the pullman-seat coffee lounges, indistinguishable from the other couples who held hands and seemed so delighted with each other's company.

Jiro's relatives were not disregarded. Arrangements were made to meet Aunt Shizu, and all were pleased to see that she acquitted herself well. Unasked, she soon expressed to Jiro her approval of Aki and her family. Formal communications were sent by mail from Aki's parents to Jiro's parents, who, after years of little use of their hands in forming Chinese characters distrusted their own ability and had their replies drafted in the schoolgirlish hand of an eighteen-year-old niece. The wedding ceremony was to be small but elegant. A lucky day was chosen, and the wedding hall of the Osaka Grand Hotel was engaged for the ceremony. With the help of Shizu, Jiro's parents were creditably dressed in rented clothing, his mother in formal black *kimono* and his father, considerably more ill at ease, in cutaway and striped trousers. Aki wore traditional bridal clothing of finest quality, complete with towering wig and the headpiece of silk that hides a bride's horns. Jiro was a fitting complement in rented morning coat and trousers. The banquet that followed was also traditional, but not the kind of wedding feast to which Jiro's parents were accustomed. The atmosphere was formal and drinking was confined to the exchange of cups required by etiquette. The bridal hall and banquet room had been reserved for use by another wedding party, due to appear as soon as the rooms had been hastily cleaned.

Jiro and Aki left for a week's honeymoon in Tokyo and scenic Nikko, which Jiro had never seen. The luxuries of the Okura Hotel, the wonders of the bursting city of Tokyo, and the poised assurance of his new bride in all of the social circumstances of the wedding and honeymoon trip deeply impressed Jiro. There were many other honeymooning couples, easy enough to identify, with whom they had exchanged sympathetic glances, but they had been happy to keep to themselves. Both were glad when the honeymoon was over, but neither felt dissatisfaction with the other. The pattern of their relationship was set. Aki would guide when guidance was needed and otherwise would follow. For his part, Jiro returned to Osaka with both affection and admiration for his wife.

Married Life

THE NEWLYWEDS   Aki's parents invited the newlyweds to live with them until they could find suitable quarters, and expected that their stay might last a year or more.

Many of the large Japanese industries owned large apartment houses, in which their employees could rent apartments at moderate fees. Asahi had no such facilities, in part because the firm had less trouble than others in attracting employees so that this fringe benefit was not regarded as necessary, and in part because its president opposed company housing. Known as one of the most progressive business executives in Japan, the president of Asahi had no objection whatever to paternalism and nepotism among the elite of the firm's officialdom so long as the men in question were otherwise competent. This he viewed as a natural and desirable state. Company housing, however, carried paternalism too far, he said, and was poor business policy except when firms erected plants in rural areas where no housing was available. The future would see all of the large and successful firms of the nation turn away from this practice, he predicted to his board of directors, because of opposition from the employees themselves. Moreover, he had shrewdly added, building and operating apartments for employees is a money-losing venture.

With gentle prompting from Aki that started almost immediately after they had taken up life in her parents' home, Jiro began looking for suitable quarters that would allow them an independent domestic life. He investigated apartments, and took Aki to see them. Led to understand that they were not suitable, he allowed Aki to take charge of the hunt. She suggested that they try one of the *danchi* built under the national housing program. The apartments in these great blocks of buildings were small, she admitted, but they were inexpensive and held many other couples like themselves. The trouble was that getting into one of the governmental *danchi* was not easy. Thousands of couples aspired to do so, and assignment was by lottery. They could at least try, she said, and they did so, unsuccessfully.

Both felt constrained living with Aki's parents and her brother's family, and they redoubled their efforts to find housing elsewhere. Widening their area of search, they found a new apartment in suburban Nigawa that was thoroughly acceptable to Jiro and tolerable to Aki. The rental fee, far too high, represented one third of Jiro's salary, newly raised after his marriage. To this monthly fee was added an enormous deposit, the equivalent of two years' rent, that the apartment owner retained as protection for his property, returning 80 per cent of the amount if the renters moved elsewhere. Unaided, there was no possibility that they could save this sum for years to come. Aware of their problem, Aki's parents offered to pay the deposit, and their offer was accepted. It was desirable that the young couple learn to be independent, but Aki was their daughter and discontent in the house affected all members.

Two months after their marriage Jiro and Aki moved into the new quarters, a two-story building of ferro-concrete painted coral and blue. Their apartment, on the second floor, had two rooms, one nine feet by eleven feet and the other six feet by nine feet, a Western toilet that made Jiro feel ill at ease for many weeks, and a Japanese bath. Entry was from an ironrailed balcony leading directly into a room floored with vinyl tile, which served as living room, kitchen, and dining room. Principal items of furniture were two basket chairs covered with tufted blue fabric, a small sofa, a lone table, and a lamp with a fluted shade. Aligned against one wall of the room was the kitchen equipment, consisting of a prefabricated unit of cupboards, drainboard, and stainless steel sink; a tiny refrigerator with a door recessed to hold bottles and four eggs; and a two-burner gas plate. Separated from the main room by sliding glass-paned doors was the bedroom, floored with reed matting in traditional style and completely devoid of furniture. The bathroom was unbelievably tiny, but they shared it with no one. All was new and shiny.

Settling down to life in their own apartment was a pleasure. Aki's knowledge of cooking stood her in good stead, and Jiro ate with evident enjoyment any food she served, Japanese or Western. Shopping was no problem. Staples were readily at hand at the old-fashioned market stalls in the nearby shopping arcade. Each tiny shop had its own specialty so that buying household foods and supplies took time; but the shopkeepers, in the old way, extended a smilingly courteous welcome that made marketing pleasant. When she was in a hurry there was always the supermarket, where the whole array of foods and household needs was assembled in a way that made shopping efficient if coldly impersonal. They lacked a telephone, which required an initial deposit far too high for them to afford, but there were many public telephones nearby and Jiro could be reached at his office.

Their first months of married life were those of a dating couple. Jiro commuted to work by electric car and subway, a trip that took an average of seventy minutes one way. After his work was finished they often met in Osaka to eat something together, see a movie, or visit an exhibition, pleasures of which Jiro had not yet tired and in which Aki was his willing companion.

To Jiro's surprise Aki often expressed sympathetic concern for his having to commute with the crowds during the rush hours. Everyone talked about the terrible congestion, of course, and one did have to be alert to avoid being crushed. There were also pickpockets to guard against. People sometimes fell in the pushing crowds in Osaka, and now and then a young woman tried to move away from the man next to her or accused him aloud of being evil. Even Jiro had to admit that the subway trip from Umeda to Namba in Osaka could be trying. People groaned, moaned, and gasped for breath under the pressure of the bodies of their fellows. In the winter, when people wore heavy suits and coats, the cries of pain were common; but the companies and offices were staggering the working hours to lighten the crush. All in all, however, Jiro enjoyed the feeling of being part of the great, busy crowd.

When they returned to their apartment late at night, the trains were uncrowded but they always contained some drunken men, sprawling about on the seats and sometimes vomiting on the floors and station platforms. The worst times were the month of December, when bonuses were paid, and much of the following month, when normal activities of the whole nation slowed to a snail's pace in celebration of New Year's. Then the late-hour drunks were a public scandal that Jiro and Aki, along with much of the rest of the nation, looked upon with distaste and disapproval as one of the inevitable but minor irritations of life.

Jiro and Aki faced a domestic problem, but of this Jiro was kept ignorant for a time. Aki quickly realized that their apartment was beyond their income, most of which was entrusted to her. Unwilling for at least a little longer to confront her husband with the unpleasant news, she had talked with her mother. Mrs. Kodama willingly supplied Aki with small funds, a few thousand *yen* each time they met, drawing the money from the secret hoard that she called her sleeve money. In the sixth month of marriage Aki learned that she was pregnant, a discovery that pleased her but also, because of their financial state, made her worry. A conference with her mother brought the ready promise of additional funds from time to time from the sleeve money and the assurance that father would, if necessary, supply more. This was not what Aki wanted, and it was not a way for her husband to win the approbation that he would need later. She made up her mind that they must find a cheaper apartment in order to retain their independence.

A talk with Jiro revealed to him their circumstances, and he was willing to follow her suggestion. They had saved no money in the brief time since their marriage, he knew, but he had not known of the over-spending. The birth of the child would automatically raise Jiro's salary slightly, but not enough for them to maintain themselves in the present apartment. A discouraging hunt for cheaper quarters followed, and then chance came to the rescue. Aki again entered the lottery for public *danchi* housing in Nigawa and this time won. As quickly as they could disentangle themselves from their obligations, they moved to the smaller and inferior, but much less expensive, apartment.

LIFE IN THE *Danchi*   Life in the *danchi* bothered Jiro not at all and caused Aki no serious discomfort. The clustered ferro-concrete buildings were large, multistoreyed, had no elevators, and looked forbidding. But they were respectable residences and within them a spirit of cheerfulness prevailed. Moreover, the Nigawa *danchi* was not one of the sprawling giants that sheltered tens of thousands of families like colonies of identical bees that rose at sunup to buzz and fly in identical ways and, as if by signal, at night became identically inert. Many of the families who shared the Nigawa *danchi* were like Jiro and Aki. The men were often college graduates, business and professional people, and some of the wives also held college degrees. Like Jiro and Aki they looked upon the *danchi* as temporary perches on the flight to finer homes. The *danchi* residents, as everyone who lived in them knew, were the people of tomorrow, the new and rising middle class of Japan.

As *danchi* residents they were kept well informed about themselves by outside observers. The Matsuis—for so Jiro and Aki had now become known—were so informed by Makita, a commercial artist who lived next door with his wife and small child. Governmental bureaus, university sociologists, and newspapers loved to investigate *danchi* and publish reports on them, particularly on the attitudes of their inhabitants. They like especially, Makita said, to prepare questionnaires to test whether we are living in the Meiji era or the twenty-first century.

Makita's statements were not far-fetched, they later learned from first-hand reading of "investigations" and second-hand reports of others. The harvest of knowledge included the information that they were young, progressive rather than traditionally minded, rationalistic, and strongly in favor of education and achievement. Their incomes placed them as solid middle class, economically above the national average. Their level of education placed them still higher socially. They were television viewers but also book lovers, acquainted with national and world affairs. They were installment buyers but financially solvent, and they were among the first to adopt time-saving instant foods and household appliances. They favored moral education for the young, looked upon all religions as much alike, and themselves generally had no faith. The *danchi* provided infertile ground for Sōka Gakkai and the other new religions, which generally drew their members from less well educated and less progressively minded sectors of the population. The *danchi* residents seldom had either Shinto votary shelves or Buddhist Butsudan in their apartments. They sometimes explained the absence of votary shelves to relatives by saying that the shelves were difficult to attach to concrete walls; sometimes religious professionals said this for them, apparently taking comfort from the explanation. The *danchi* residents often did not care very much whether or not their family lines were carried on by male heirs, and aged parents rarely lived with them even when there was room. Jiro and Aki found little in these descriptions that seemed inaccurate.

Even the predictions they heard and read about *danchi* residents of the future seemed reasonable. The young, it was said, found life in the housing developments tolerable or even pleasant. As they grew to middle age, the monotonous uniformity and pressures toward conformity of *danchi* life would become intolerable for many. After a few years, as new developments were added, the character of the *danchi* residents would change. Regulations allowed admission only to families with incomes above a moderate minimum and thus the early *danchi* people were of middle class. Rising incomes were even now bringing in industrial workers and others of lower social class than the first wave. The completion a few years hence of super-*danchi*, planned to house not tens but hundreds of thousands, would find the developments inhabited by great colonies of working class families.

Two months after they moved into the *danchi*, Aki gave birth to their daughter Emi. By this time she had made friends with several neighbors, pregnant like herself or the mothers of young children. The birth, in a hospital, had been untroubled, and Jiro had shown no disappointment that their child was a daughter. They both hoped to have one more child, preferably a son but a daughter would also be welcome. The child was normal and healthy, but it was soon clear that Aki could not provide all the nourishment the infant required. At their doctor's recommendation, bottles, nipples, and a sterilizer were purchased, and Emi became one of several dozen infants in the *danchi* living on a supplementary diet.

Domestic finance was considerably aided by gifts for the baby from Aki's parents and other relatives. Jiro's parents sent a brilliantly colored infant's *kimono*, in country style, which was placed in a drawer and never worn. Recreation for Jiro and Aki now consisted of television turned down to a whisper, books and magazines, occasional chats with neighbors, visits with the relatives, and enjoyment of the baby. Jiro sometimes helped with the housework and felt no loss of masculinity for doing so.

Aki had never visited Takashima and Jiro had not been there for several years. When Jiro's parents expressed a wish to see their new grandchild, Aki said that it was their duty to take the child to Takashima and added, honestly enough, that she would like to make the trip. The visit was brief and none too comfortable. Aki and Emi were well received, and Aki in her usual way was friendly and gracious. But there was an atmosphere of reserve that was especially evident when they met Jiro's more distant relatives and former neighbors. Beyond greetings, expressed in the vocabulary of country courtesy, those outside Jiro's family had found nothing to say to the visitors. The trip was Aki's first close contact with country people other than acquaintance with various maids from the country in the employ of her family and the families of friends. Like most urban Japanese she had thought of rural residents as people apart. She found the scenery beautiful, the houses and farm plots picturesque, the food coarse, and the people quaint and timid but worthy. Jiro's ideas had become much the same, and both returned to Osaka with the secret feeling of a duty performed.

Marriage and fatherhood brought no neglect by Jiro of his duties at Asahi. His salary was coming along, and men in authority addressed him in ways that showed regard. Within the large organization there were many internecine jealousies, of which he was as yet less fully aware than others. For this reason he could honestly treat with open pleasantness even those who might look upon him with jealousy. It had become clear since the time of his marriage that he was being watched with special attention and that his prospects for advancement were good. The affability and pliancy that had been his traits all through life were assets. He was appraised by those above him as a man who knew all the rules and caused no discord, a man intensely loyal to the interests of the department and firm, one who could be implicitly trusted to carry out orders efficiently, and one who, when so requested, could direct the completion of tasks by others without causing friction. As an approver with intelligence, ability, a prepossessing appearance, and ties with well-placed officials, there was a good place for him.

IN TOKYO   When Emi was nearly two years old, Jiro was taken one day by Mr. Kodama, his department chairman and now his uncle, to the office of one of Asahi's two executive directors, where he was informed that he would have new duties that brought a substantial promotion. The new post required that he and his family move to Tokyo, but his salary would be adjusted to compensate for the higher cost of living there. As they left the director's office, Mr. Kodama explained that it made for better relations in the firm if people who received such substantial promotions were moved to different offices, at least for a time. Dazed by his good fortune, Jiro brought the news home to Aki, who took it with composure and began immediately to make plans for moving to Tokyo.

Asahi Industries had begun in Osaka and remained an Osaka firm. Like other large industries of Japan, it maintained important offices in Tokyo. Like the heads of various other large Osaka firms, Asahi's president found it useful to spend most of his time in Tokyo, close to the heads of the other large industries of the nation and close to the offices of the national government. When Jiro arrived in Tokyo he was informed that the president would see him. Ushered into his presence for a brief word of welcome, Jiro knew that he had received a stamp of approval.

Tokyo is very much to Jiro's liking. Their apartment, resembling the one they had briefly occupied in Nishinomiya, is far more expensive, but they can now afford it. The immediate neighborhood is good, but they must take care after dark. To avoid the possibility of trouble from juvenile delinquents or members of gangs of adult criminals who occasionally drift into the area at night, it is best to ride by taxi from the electric train station to the apartment after eight o'clock. These are ordinary precautions that women in particular should be careful to take.

With Aki's sympathy Jiro still rides public vehicles to and from work, in crowds still denser than in Osaka. As before, they hold no terror for him. Tokyo is quite as exciting as he had remembered it from their honeymoon. Well received by associates at Asahi, Jiro quickly felt himself a part of the group. Even lunch, with friendly companions, is an adventure. Work at the office and home life at night do not allow much time for exploration of Tokyo, but it is pleasant to know that the riches of the city are available. Skiing has been forsaken as a pastime of his carefree youth, but he has kept his skiing equipment and sometimes feels pangs of nostalgia when he sees the long queues of youthful skiers at the railroad stations. Jiro and Aki have become acquainted with their neighbors to the point of exchanging cordial greetings, but they have so far declined to join the Neighborhood Association. Jiro's ties are with Asahi, which, together with his family, provide all the companionship he needs.

Aki's view of Tokyo is less enthusiastic than Jiro's, but she knows the move is right for their future. The air, even dirtier than in Osaka and foul as compared with that of Nishinomiya, begrimes clothes in a few hours, and travel about the city by public transportation is uncomfortable and exhausting. The needs of daily life may all be purchased in the immediate neighborhood of the apartment, however, and there is little reason for Aki to travel. Social life is satisfactory, if, so far, less active than in Osaka. Aki has an uncle in Tokyo, whom they sometimes visit, and there are other social affairs in connection with Jiro's work. Now and then, in the company of her aunt, Aki attends concerts, lectures, or fashion shows of clothing by the famous French and Italian couturiers. The clothes are beyond her means but nonetheless enjoyable to see.

Aki is biding her time. Her hopes are for a home of their own, in Tokyo if necessary but preferably near Osaka. There is no hope of their owning a house near the heart of Tokyo, where the cost of real estate is fantastic. A century of Jiro's present salary would be required to buy a house like that of her parents in Nishinomiya. On the far outskirts of the city, hours by train, they may buy a house for the equivalent of only five or six years of his earnings, a small, new house set out in the middle of farmers' fields or in a development with many similar houses. One of these will do, but Aki's heart is back at home. She does not doubt that they will return to Osaka, and she is confident that Jiro will rise to a position that will provide them comfort and a home of their own in the suburbs of Osaka, perhaps even in Ashiya, the finest place in all Japan. These are matters in which she can help.

Top: The island and community of Takashima in 1951, before the area of sea between Takashima and the mainland (in the foreground) was filled in.

Bottom: Takashima in late 1974 (wooded eminence in background), after the strip of sea had been filled in with earth and sand and had become the site of industrial plants.

4

An Urbanized Rural Community

The City of Kurashiki

Since the end of World War II thousands of small, once rural Japanese communities have become incorporated in industrial cities. Old and great industrial centers such as Tokyo and Osaka have spread so that their margins have become bedrooms for urban commuters or sites of industrial plants. New industrial cities have also arisen. The city of Kurashiki, in Okayama Prefecture on the Inland Sea, is one of these. Until recent years Kurashiki was a small, provincial city known principally for traditional architecture, pottery making and other folk crafts, and three museums of folk art, archeology, and fine arts. Before the 1960s, the only large industries in Kurashiki were spinning mills, which produced the wealth allowing the establishment of the museums. Outstanding among these is the Ohara Fine Arts Museum, a building with a classic Greek facade which houses principally Western oil paintings, including a large collection of works by French impressionists.

In the 1950s the city began its growth into what is now the fifth largest industrial complex in the nation. A deep ships' channel was dredged in the shallow waters of the Inland Sea to allow the construction of an international port; a large area of swampy or submerged seaside land was reclaimed, and the municipal leaders began a campaign of courting large industrial firms of the nation to establish manufacturing plants in the newly reclaimed area. New industries by the dozens erected large factories there in the 1960s. In 1975, the population of Kurashiki was about 400,000 people.

During the period of its industrial development, Kurashiki continued at an accelerated rate an old program of annexation of neighboring communities. The greatest addition was in 1967, when the entire neighboring city of Kojima, with a population of about 100,000 people, was annexed. As a part of Kojima, Takashima then became a community of Kurashiki.

The modern city of Kurashiki is visually a combination of rural and

91

urban scenes. New industry is concentrated principally in the reclaimed area, called Mizushima, where land was available and where port facilities suitable for large ships were constructed. Included among the industrial plants are oil refineries, many chemical plants, an automobile factory, a huge steel company, cement factories, a shipbuilding firm, and much else. Textile and clothing manufacturing concerns are concentrated in the former city of Kojima, some miles from Mizushima, where they were established many years ago. Elsewhere, rice fields, geographically isolated hamlets, and low hills break up the nearly 300 square kilometers of the city's area. This rural-looking part of the city is threaded by highways and varied here and there by large clusters of high-rise apartments, principally *danchi* owned by the industrial firms of Mizushima and occupied by their employees. Traffic on the city's roads is heavy, and the main arteries become glutted by the addition of many private cars during the morning and evening rush hours. Travel is nevertheless ordinarily rapid, and city bus lines are well developed.

Insofar as modern conditions will allow, old Kurashiki—the site of the original city and still the municipal center—is preserved in its past form, thereby constituting another economic enterprise. Crowds of tourists congest the museums and the area of the old city where the handsome, antique dwellings with black and white exteriors are the most abundant and best preserved. Hungry for diversion, the tourists also travel by bus within the city to view the Inland Sea from the Skyline Drive and visit the Mizushima industrial area and several undistinguished temples and shrines.

The process of expansion has brought Kurashiki's territorial limits within a few miles of the city of Okayama, with a population of about 500,000. A regional city of importance since ancient times and the capitol of the prefecture, Okayama followed a pattern of growth similar to but slower than that of Kurashiki. The two neighboring cities and their immediately adjoining areas thus compose an urbanized area inhabited by about one million people within which exist a network of roads and a heavily used railroad.

As a rapidly industrialized city, Kurashiki drew a large part of its added population from elsewhere. Trained specialists and technicians came from Tokyo, Osaka, and other large cities. Since locally available labor was untrained and inadequate in quantity, many skilled and unskilled workmen were drawn from other and sometimes far-flung parts of the nation, as remote as Okinawa and Hokkaido, wherever labor was available and wherever individual industrial firms were best able to recruit workmen. About 60 percent of the employees of one large chemical plant, for example, came from southern Kyushu, several hundred miles away, where the firm in question operates one of its many large factories. Except for a temporary rise in the crime rate at the time of the heaviest activity of construction of the industrial plants, when many imported construction workers were in the city temporarily, the growth of the community was peaceful. Today, about two-thirds of Kurashiki's people are native residents of Okayama prefecture. These include a few thousand *burakumin* and a smaller number of Koreans, groups that are small and with whom most Kurashiki residents have no contact or no witting contact. Only a handful of

Europeans and Americans are permanent residents, but, as tourists or visiting businessmen, a sprinkling of these foreigners is always present.

Except for the unusual speed of its industrialization, Kurashiki has a modern history much like that of various other industrial centers of Japan. The effects of industrialization in raising incomes and standards of living and otherwise altering conditions of life of the city's population are essentially the same as elsewhere in the nation. One change—usually ruefully called a consequence—is especially worthy of note because it had strong influence on the community of Takashima. Kurashiki has suffered heavily from environmental pollution. Since its industrialization had been unusually rapid, environmental pollution came to the city with similar speed. But this history is better related as it applies to Takashima, one of the communities of the city which was most drastically affected by environmental pollution as well as by other effects of rapid industrialization.

The Industrialization of Takashima

Ten years ago, Takashima was still a fishing community. Untrained in any other occupation, its fishermen continued their old occupation. Since the price of fish rose as economic conditions of the nation brightened, local incomes also rose, and served as an added incentive to continue fishing. Fears about the future began turning into reality very quickly after the factories were constructed at Mizushima, which at first adjoined and, with further expansion of the industrial area, later came to include Takashima on its periphery.

Foul-smelling fish appeared in the nets in the mid-1960s and catches declined. Other fishing communities in the area reported similar problems, and newspapers carried articles about the existence of mercury, waste oil, cadmium and other harmful substances in the sea. A few of the younger Takashima fishermen then took employment with Mizushima firms, but most men continued to fish as best they could. In 1968 the first factory, a chemical plant, was erected on the landfill, completed a few years earlier, that had once been a strip of sea between Takashima and the mainland. Other industrial plants very quickly followed, and environmental pollution mounted. A giant steel plant nearby visibly emitted acrid, sulphurous fumes day and night, and it was certain that effluents of other industrial plants were making the water and air increasingly foul. The once abundant clams on the remaining seaward beaches of the former island disappeared. Curiously malformed fish were seen from time to time. People began to talk of having difficulty in breathing and sleeping and to seek medical aid for these problems.

Other changes that anyone could see were equally ominous. Weakened by sulphur fumes, the many large pine trees on the hill behind the settlement were killed by boring insects, and a luxurious growth of poison sumac, formerly uncommon in Takashima, appeared in replacement. Bamboo and some vegetables grew poorly, failing to sprout or to mature, or did not grow at all. Except for the crows and the sparrows, even the birds disappeared, leaving behind them an ugly wasteland of dead and dying pine trees in a setting of grimly functional manufacturing plants.

By 1970 several industrial plants had been constructed near Takashima and pollution had increased to the point that remedial action of some kind was thought to be necessary or else the people would be forced to leave the community. The local fishermen's cooperative association joined other fishermen's cooperatives and citizens' groups in clamoring for aid, stating their cases before city officials and local heads of industrial plants. In 1972, the city of Kurashiki engaged a team of sociologists to make a survey of conditions of life in Takashima and two other former hamlets, the three communities of the city that appeared to have been most seriously affected by environmental pollution, which, by now, everyone called *kōgai*, "public damage," although other words literally meaning environmental pollution exist. This investigation reported what everyone already knew, that pollution was severe and that the people were apprehensive about both livelihood and health.

Similar problems in many other cities had by this time led to various steps of governmental action at national, prefectural, and city levels, to which news media gave much attention. Physical examinations of presumably afflicted people were conducted. In some cities, such as Minamata, on the island of Kyushu, a disease caused by industrial effluents was firmly diagnosed. Elsewhere, a pathology of the bones caused by cadmium became nationally known as the "ouch ouch disease." In Takashima, one woman who suffered from a respiratory problem diagnosed as asthma was declared a *nintei kanja*, official invalid, whose medical bills were to be paid by the city.

In Kurashiki, as in other cities, legislation was enacted to control the harmful activities of industrial plants, and compensatory funds, administered by the prefectural government but said to be derived in part from industrial firms, were paid to people who had suffered financial losses as the result of environmental pollution. For Takashima people, payments consisted at first of several relatively small sums to compensate for damage to fishing only. In 1973, fishing stopped entirely in the waters available to Takashima fishermen, with no hope of its resumption at a later date. In early 1974 the fishermen's cooperative association to which Takashima fishermen belonged was officially disbanded as being useless. Before dissolution, the cooperative had agreed with prefectural officials upon a final compensation to be paid to its members for permanent loss of their source of livelihood. The sum, about $47,000 for each full-time fisherman, seemed stunningly large to its recipients, most of whom had never imagined themselves as possessors of even a fraction of such wealth.

The immediate future was then secure, but many years of life lay ahead. During the 1960s and especially after the annexation by Kurashiki in 1967, incomes had risen, and former luxuries fairly quickly became necessities. Telephones, refrigerators, and gas stoves were all in this class, and private cars were so regarded by many people. Their children should go to high school, of course, and they really should go on to college. The old days of scrabbling for a living, of doing such things as mixing lowly barley with rice, raising one's own vegetables and chickens, and eating great quantities of home-grown sweet potatoes were gone. Everyone knew Takashima had become an eyesore, and some people now and then expressed a longing for the old days of clean air and sea and flourishing pine trees, but no able-bodied man or woman wished to return to the past and no livelihood could possibly be gained from the resources in Takashima.

The obvious answer was to find industrial employment, which nearly everyone was willing and even eager to do. The problem was where to find it. Mizushima industrial firms followed the policies of other large firms of the nation. They would rarely accept people over age 35 as regular employees, that is, as personnel qualifying for retirement and other fringe benefits as well as for "lifetime" employment, and their regular employees were retired at age 55. Moreover, the industrial firms had little interest in men and women with only 6 to 9 years of formal education. Many Takashima men and women failed to meet the requirements of both age and education. A man or woman could, however, take temporary employment, subject to layoff at any time, with some of the large firms and, more easily, with the many small firms associated with the large concerns as subcontractors. These small firms paid less, of course, and were in other ways less desirable as employers, but, as long as national economic conditions were favorable, continued employment with them could be expected. The great hope was a shipbuilding firm which, purchasing a small piece of land from Takashima people, constructed its yard on this land, an adjacent area of landfill, and into the sea at one end of the former island.

Beginning operations in January 1974, the firm was receptive to Takashima people as applicants for employment, accepting as trainees for regular employment several men in their late 30s and early 40s as well as younger men and women. Forty-two men and women entered the employment of either the main firm or its various subcontractors, which performed specialized tasks such as painting and ironwork. In early 1975, every able-bodied male under 60 years of age was gainfully employed except one, an acknowledged, lifelong ne'er-do-well, who did not seek industrial employment. With rare exception, able-bodied women of the same range of ages were also employed, either full or part time. Young men and men in early middle age quickly became semiskilled and skilled workmen—ironworkers, welders, instrument operators, and the like. Most men who were 40 or older took employment with subcontractors, and the older of these men were given the least desirable work, as common laborers. Middle-aged women employed by the new industrial firms became food handlers, serving lunches to employees, and janitors. A double handful of men and women, generally young, held clerical positions, in industrial firms and elsewhere. A small number of people had still other occupations, as independent carpenter, ship's crew member, box factory operator, custodian in municipal offices, and as gas station attendant. A few people, principally women, operated small inns and restaurants or aided relatives in doing so. Only one person, a trained civil engineer who married a Takashima girl, was in the professional class. No one today holds gainful employment that can be called rural, and more than three-fourths of the working population are employed by industrial firms. The kitchen farming of the past is now a part-time activity done principally by aged men and women, partly as a hobby and partly as a way of making themselves feel worthwhile.

The year 1974 was a turning point in the conditions of environmental pollution. The threat of disaster then appeared to have become much less ominous, and assurance had been given by city officials that further helpful steps would be taken. Some of the birds returned that year and the garden vegetables seemed healthy. The ocean was still polluted, and smoke often hung' in the air, but the sulphurous smells of earlier years had gone. City officials of Kurashiki then stopped making public clamor about environmental pollution, as did the people of Takashima and other afflicted communities. The reasons were clearly stated. It was deemed economically and otherwise undesirable to advertise Kurashiki as a city deeply troubled by *kōgai*. If, like Minamata and other badly affected cities, the name Kurashiki became synonymous with environmental pollution, growth of the city would stop. As one of the local heights of affliction, Takashima would similarly suffer. In particular, its people thought that no brides could possibly be attracted to such a place—and the young men would then inevitably leave.

The year 1974 was a turning point in other ways. All employable people had found employment. Although inflation was a source of great worry, nearly every family owned a house and a little land, now very valuable; familial incomes were greater than at any time in the past; and standards of living had continued to rise despite inflation. For many families, the sum of money paid to the former fishermen as their last compensation, most of which now rested safely in banks and other financial institutions, constituted a warmly comforting hedge against future poverty.

The history of Takashima in the past decade includes many events beyond those described above. The transition to industrial employment and suburban life brought changes in social relations, family composition, and in every other aspect of existence. To understand some of these it is necessary to know a little more of the physical features of the community and its human composition.

By 1975 Takashima had become a residential island, separated from the nearest neighboring community by a half-mile of industrial plants. The entrance to Takashima had become a four-lane highway, replete with a dividing island and bordered by sidewalks and planted camphor trees. The highway ends at what was formerly the beach lying in front of the settlement. This area is now the site of a large, modern fire station operated by the city, a restaurant, and, to the left side, the new shipyard. Immediately above the houses stand three multistoried buildings of ferro-concrete, the offices of the shipbuilding firm, the combined offices of this firm's subcontractors, and a Western style guesthouse erected by the shipbuilding company as a hostel for the crew members of foreign ships that would in the future come to its yard for repairs. A sturdy chain-link fence separates these buildings and their grounds from the Takashima residences and kitchen gardens, and it is clearly understood without further notification that movement past the fence in either direction is trespass. The terraced kitchen gardens, reduced to about one-fifth of the size they were

10 or 15 years ago, are succeeded on higher slopes by a tangle of poison sumac and other low and hardy vegetation from which the skeletons of pine trees protrude. Atop the hill behind the settlement stands a lighthouse, erected in 1974, that warns the hundreds of ships daily using the Mizushima channel of the presence of land. On the seaward side of the former island an immense collection of buildings and the cokeyard of a steel company thrust a gradually lengthening arm into the sea, leaving as open water only the ships' channel between the plant and Takashima. To the right stretch miles of Mizushima industrial plants. The air is full of smoke, the vista limited and bleak.

Social Changes in Takashima

The human community of Takashima is essentially intact. Losses of people during the past ten years have been principally "normal" losses, the kinds of outflow that applied in Japan in pre-industrial times. A few people have died, and those who have moved to other communities consist chiefly of a long succession of young women who left at the time of their marriage and a much smaller number of second and third sons. Few entire families have left, and only two small families of outsiders, presumed to be temporary residents, have moved into Takashima, as renters. Several people who had moved to Osaka or other cities during the past 30 years have made a U-turn to live in Takashima. The population has increased by 12 persons, rising from 188 to 200. The birth rate is very low, less than one-half the rate of 15 years ago, a circumstance that the people explain as the result of planning. Only 16 children are under 10 years of age, whereas 46 children range in age from 10 to 19 years. At the other end of the lifespan the number of people has increased and, as judged by conditions of health, will soon grow much larger. The oldest resident, a woman, is 97, and 34 people are 60 years of age or older. A dozen people are described by an ancient humorous expression as those who have "forgotten how to die."

Families have shrunk in size, to an average of four persons. Dwellings have correspondingly grown in number from 33 to 51. Five old women and one old man live alone, by their own choice. As these conditions suggest, familial relations have also changed. Multigenerational families under a single roof grow less and less common. Talk still exists of *honke* and *bunke*, main and branch houses, but these terms now only inform that the families are lineally related. Whenever financial circumstances have permitted, new dwellings have been erected for sons at the time of their marriage, and sometimes these have been eldest sons, the traditional heirs to their parents' homes and lands. Unless their families have considerable wealth, young men who plan or are expected to live with their parents after they marry suffer from the national ailment for their class: few young women wish to marry them.

The small family of parents and children is tightly united, but circumstances increasingly discourage close ties with other relatives and neighbors. Friendships come more easily and satisfactorily through other channels, of school and places of employment. Although most Takashima people are some-how relatives, few of the young know the nature of their kinship with many of their more distant kin and, each year, know less about their lives. The terms "uncle," "aunt," "elder sister," and "elder brother" are no longer frequently used to address distant kin or unrelated neighbors, although any old person is still ordinarily called "grandmother" or "grandfather."

Common-interest associations have also changed greatly, but they show no signs of weakening. Much of the community solidarity of former times was achieved through these associations. Solidarity has progressively weakened for the same reasons as apply to ramified ties of kinship, but, as a form of social grouping, the associations appear to be stronger than ever. The major change has been that most of the associations to which Takashima people belong today are not limited in their membership to Takashima people, and, for this reason, they disfavor rather than favor community solidarity.

The appearance and demise of the common-interest associations causes no disturbance to kin groups and no disturbances of other kinds of which the people are aware, since they rise and fall to meet the occasion. Various associa-tions have disappeared because their roles were assumed by municipal, pre-fectural, and national agencies, commercial institutions of credit and insurance, and new ways of finding pleasurable human associations and activities of recreation. The young people's association had been the first of the old ones to go, twenty years ago, for loss of practical roles and because of the existence of more suitable opportunities to create friendships with outsiders. The women's association collapsed in the 1970s after existing only nominally for some years, and the fire prevention association, its role assumed by the city fire station, exists today in name only. As occupations changed, the fishermen's cooperative ceased to have relevance and disbanded. As kitchen farming—once involving some sale of cash crops—ceased to be important, so also did membership in the farmers' cooperative, which retains only a small spark of life in Takashima. The funeral association has lost most of its tasks to telephones and catering firms. In former times, its important tasks when deaths occurred included giving verbal notification of the deaths in person—there was no other way—to the local priest and to relatives of the deceased living in other communities. Another task was the preparation of food for the bereaved and for guests at the funeral. This association, now divided into two groups to accord better with the increased number of households, still exists, perhaps principally because the traditional funeral service calls for nonrelatives to fill certain ceremonial roles.

The hamlet association, formerly the most important group in com-munity affairs, has lost to the municipal administration many of its old func-tions, such as maintenance of the community roads and water supply. This association retains some life, especially in connection with maintenance and supervision of community property, of which the graveyard is the most im-portant item. But meetings are few today and leadership of this association, once an honor, is accepted only with reluctance as an irksome civic duty.

Only one of the old associations, the P.T.A., has retained vigor and, if anything, it now has added vigor. All parents of children in the single elementary school participate actively in its P.T.A., and many parents participate in the associations of the various junior high schools, some miles away, which their children attend. The transition from fishing to industrial employment gave a memorable lesson about the importance of formal education. Any juvenile or adult in Takashima knows who among the young people of the community is attending college, even though their given names may be unknown, and everyone also knows who attends the special cram schools in Okayama City in preparation for taking college entrance examinations.

As old associations have disappeared, others have arisen that fit the modern scene, and membership in most of these new groups bring the people in greater contact with the world outside Takashima and lesser contact with their kin and neighbors. A voluntary association of Takashima residents was active for a time in dealing with problems of environmental pollution, until its efforts resulted in the pursuit of its goal by city and prefectural agencies. Two important kinds of associations have recently risen to prominence. One of these is labor unions, with which Takashima people, as new members, are not yet very familiar. All "permanent" employees of large industrial firms belong to company labor unions. Whether regular or temporary, employees of these firms may belong to the second kind of new association, the company clubs concerned with sports, esthetics, and other activities of leisure time.

A casual look at religious activities suggests greater religiosity. Like other formerly impoverished people of Japan, the residents of Takashima have bought new and expensive Buddhist altars, and funerals have become so elaborate that the wife of the local priest describes them as gaudy. The use of catering firms to supply food for mourners, the chartering of buses to convey mourners to the crematorium for the final rite of the funeral, and the presence of three priests at a funeral when one might serve quite adequately are not traditional customs of Takashima, and, as elsewhere in Japan, they appear to be effects of economic prosperity and examples of conspicuous consumption.

Many of the aged people are indeed traditionally religious, but even they cannot preserve religious customs related to fishing, farming, and health since the customs have little or no meaning today. The young often do not know the names of many of the traditional rites. Shingon Buddhism is still the religion of most members of the community, whose religious acts are generally limited to participation in funerals and commemorative rites for deceased relatives. The local priest, in the nearby community of Shionasu, has prospered enough in recent years to allow him to resign from his position as elementary school teacher. He is careful to visit each family twice yearly, at New Year's and O-Bon in late summer, the only two annual festival occasions of importance to the nation. He is also careful to remind people by postcard of dates when commemorative ceremonies for ancestors should be held.

Shinto folk beliefs and customs have fared less well than Buddhism. The shrine of Kōjinsama, the tutelary god of Takashima, that lies up the hill behind the dwellings is rarely visited by anyone except a few old women. Out of deference to them, however, the shrine is maintained by the community association. Ebisusama, the god of fishermen, died in 1974. Following a heavy mid-summer rain, a miniature landslide crushed the small wooden structure in which he was enshrined but left undamaged the ancient, carved wooden representation of the god. Since fishing had ended, no efforts were made to repair or replace the structure, and the statue of Ebisusama was left exposed to the hot sun and rain. Three months later the statue disappeared, presumably into the hands of a passerby, a fancier of antiques.

Most of the ancient Shinto customs have only a glimmer of life, among the aged. Such beliefs and practices as those concerning pollution and taboo are unfamiliar even to the middle-aged. But here and there a few old customs survive. Before a house is built, the old ceremony of consecrating the ground is observed, and, if finances will allow, a ceremony involving the lavish distribution of rice cakes is held when the framework of a house is erected. In 1974, a protective ceremony called by the ancient name *o-harai*, literally "exorcism," was conducted at the opening for the summer of the swimming pool at a junior high school attended by a number of Takashima children, and a second ceremony, bearing the same name but said to be a rite of thanks, was conducted when the pool was closed at the end of summer. Beliefs about auspicious and inauspicious days, calendrical years, years of life, and directions of the compass are far from dead. These, however, are not ordinarily regarded as religion but, dependent upon one's degree of faith in them, as superstitions or simply beliefs.

Something nominally new has been added in the realm of religion. Two families, totaling seven persons, joined the religious sect Sōka Gakkai after the community was subjected to intensive proselytizing in 1964 and 1965. Most Takashima people oppose Sōka Gakkai on the grounds that it is a militant, exclusive sect that aims to control the nation politically as well as in every other way. The Takashima converts, well aware of this opinion, are apologetic or secretive about their affiliation with the sect. They are nevertheless faithful in attending the weekly meetings of the sect, which are held in rotation at the homes of the few members in Takashima and several other small residential communities nearby.

Daily life in Takashima today is an aggregate of the many kinds of lives in which the five generations of its people were reared. The oldest can remember the nineteenth century. A few of the eldest women are illiterate; the young who are now in high school generally expect to attend college. Whether people are young or old, their prevailing way of life is suburban, a life of alarm clocks, work schedules, automobiles, television, banks, insurance policies, labor unions, and international forms of entertainment. The aged as well as the middle-aged have adjusted and will doubtless continue to adjust.

The economic changes described in the preceding pages have unquestionably altered conditions of life in a way that has greatly weakened community solidarity. At the same time, however, they have fortuitously brought conditions that favor the continued existence of Takashima as a socially distinct community with some degree of unity. One of these conditions is the geographical isolation of the community imposed by the presence of industrial plants, which is unlikely to change. Few outsiders desire to move into such an unattractive community, and Takashima residents are reluctant to sell such small parcels of their land as are suitable for the construction of dwellings. They have seen the value of land and buildings rise thousands of percent in the past thirty years, and their view is that land can only increase in value. The people of Takashima expect to remain in Takashima. Moving elsewhere, they realize, would lower rather than raise their standard of living. They are well aware that their homes, once poor by national standards, are today superior to the average in spaciousness and, often, in their facilities. These circumstances added to the bonds of kinship, now weakened but nevertheless somehow valued, foster the continued survival of Takashima for some years as a community with some degree of in-group sentiment.

The Actors, Yesterday and Today

All of the principal figures in the narratives written a decade ago are alive. The urban family is confirmedly urban. Jiro and Aki have the ideal family of two children, a boy and a girl, and are careful to see that their family grows no larger. Jiro has a secure position with his firm and is regarded as valuable if not creative. Transferred back to the home office in Osaka after several years in Tokyo, he was given a housing allowance permitting the rental of an expensive apartment complete with central heat, carpeting, and what was called a "dream kitchen." The ideal home in nearby Ashiya did not become a reality, but Jiro and Aki are content with what they have. Aki's father and mother died in quick succession, willing to her their home, which Aki's affluent sisters and her brother did not want or need. Remodeling, especially of the kitchen and living room, gave them a home better than any they could buy and, fortunately, the remodeling was done in 1970, before the worst of the inflation came.

Jiro has not returned to Takashima for seven years and does not plan to go there again unless there is a death among members of his family. He telephones his parents and Aunt Shizu frequently and he has often invited them to visit him and his family. Shizu accepts and, to the enjoyment of all, makes at least one visit annually. But Jiro's parents do not know what to do with themselves at his home, and Jiro and Aki are equally troubled in finding ways to make them enjoy themselves. After two visits soon after Jiro had returned to Osaka, they have not accepted their son's invitations.

Our erstwhile rural family is now a suburban family. Hajime, the household head, is 54; Hanako, his wife, is 49. Both have been employed for a year by Asaki Ironworks, a small subsidiary of the Takashima shipbuilding firm, Hajime as a general helper and cleanup man, and his wife as a food handler. Hajime is not fond of his work but is quite willing to do it. After nearly thirty years of life as a housewife, Hanako enjoys her work and the human associations it brings.

Akira, the eldest son, now 26, lives at home but is seldom there except to sleep and eat breakfast. After finishing high school, he worked with his father and grandfather for two years as a fisherman before deciding that no future lay in that occupation. He then applied for employment at a new chemical plant in Mizushima, three miles from home, and was immediately accepted as a trainee for whatever work seemed best suited to the firm's concerns and his abilities. A permanent employee for three years now, he supervises an instrument panel that controls the time and temperature of various chemical processes of manufacturing ethylene and other chemicals. He knows that he can expect to rise little higher in the occupational hierarchy because the really good positions are held almost entirely by college graduates. But his salary is good; semiannual bonuses paid by his prosperous firm are generous, and he likes his work. He explains that, unlike fishing, his present work requires the use of his head. The owner of a car for two years, Akira commutes to work, and often does not return home in the evening. He is then careful to telephone his parents to say that he will spend the night with bowling companions.

Akira expects to look after the welfare of his parents when they can no longer work and perhaps also to care for his grandparents, who are now 79 and 75 but in fine health. He does not regard this commitment as an intolerable burden but rather as an undesirable but none too extraordinary role, a moral obligation, that has fallen to him as well as to many other men. The burden will not be very heavy financially since his parents have saved considerable money but it might be difficult in another way if his parents and grandparents live for many years in senility. Tales about the behavior of Masako, the old widow who lives nearby with her son and his family, worry all aged and aging people and all those who live or expect to live with aged relatives. Masako seems healthy but her mind has been tangled for years. She sees remarkable things that no one else has ever seen, such as foxes darting about in the gardens and roads, and fire trucks and ambulances atop the hill where no road exists. These visions are only slightly troublesome and, as everyone knows, they come to many old people. Masako is always gentle, but on the days when the past becomes the present, her behavior is very troublesome. She wanders about without sensible destination and must be watched carefully. Sometimes, in response to worried telephone calls from shops miles away, she must be taken into protective custody. A tremulous bride-to-be, she disturbs the clerks by selecting fabrics for her bridal clothing. At other times she does such things as select infant's clothing for the expected arrival of her first child.

Akira's grandfather and grandmother live apart from their offspring in quarters consisting of two pleasant rooms that were built near the main house nearly ten years ago. They spend little time at the bigger house and are careful to choose appropriate times to make calls. Much of their waking time is spent in cultivating the family vegetable plot, now reduced in size, and, at their house, in raising potted plants, watching television, and providing companionship for each other. Money is not a worry. As a full-time fisherman despite his age, grandfather received $47,000 as his final compensation. Placed in a savings account, this sum provides interest large enough to meet the simple living requirements of his wife and himself. Since both are over 70 years of age, medical services are available to them without cost according to national law. Akira's father, Hajime, also received the same compensation of $47,000, and spent only a little of it to remodel the kitchen of his home. In its new form the kitchen has vinyl floor covering, a stainless steel sink and drainboard, hot water supplied by a tank heated by propane gas, a propane stove with two burners and a broiling compartment, many wall cabinets for storage, a refrigerator with a freezer compartment, and, for use in the hot weather, an electric room cooler.

In due time, Akira will inherit all of the valuable family property and have a good home. His sister Yuriko, now 24, is married and lives in central Kurashiki. Accepting as her inheritance a lavish wedding, conducted at a wedding hall in Okayama City, and a very generous trousseau, she is satisfied.

The future of little Makoto, Akira's brother and the youngest child in the family, will be cared for in another way. Now 15 and a high school student, little Makoto is no longer little; nearly six feet tall, he is the giant of the family. Makoto has always been a zealous student, and his future seems assured. He will go to college, and from all present indications he will be able to pass the entrance examinations of a fine one.

As a whole Akira looks upon his circumstances as fortunate. Some of his family's neighbors have fared better but others far more poorly. He knows that the financial fortunes of Masaichi and his family have soared to new heights. Now 70, Masaichi is still the head of his household, still the community's only truly effective representative in relations with the city and the rest of the world outside Takashima, and still disliked despite general acknowledgement of his value to the community. No one knows much about Masaichi's affairs since fishing ended, but it is certain that he is always busy and makes many trips to central Kurashiki. Gossip, which takes place at a restaurant-beer parlor operated by Takashima women, holds that he is now a businessman and an investor in the stock market.

At the other extreme there is Sei-ichi, who grew up with Akira's father. Always carefree and indolent, his greatest achievement was to become manager and part owner of a pinball parlor, which promptly went bankrupt. Idling the days away, Sei-ichi cannot find employment and has no income beyond an occasional windfall from pinball playing and illegal gambling. He and his family subsist thinly on the earnings of his wife, who handles all domestic tasks of a large family and, in such time as she can find, earns money by the machine sewing of clothing for a firm that similarly employs other housebound Takashima women. The lives of Sei-ichi and his family are further complicated by Sei-ichi's aged father, who, refusing to receive free medical care at a hospital, is dying a lingering death at home from tuberculosis contracted many years ago.

As compared with the lot of Sei-ichi and his family, Akira regards his circumstances as fortunate, but he is troubled by a familiar problem and it grows a little larger daily. At 26, it is time for him to marry. Last year his parents hesitantly suggested that a bride could be found through a go-between, if he so wished. Akira replied briefly that he would find a wife himself—and there the matter rested. Akira is personable, sociable, and at ease in the presence of women. His free time is often spent in the company of girls, and he has found two in whom he has had special interest. So far, he has met no one suiting his tastes who has expressed any interest whatever in an alliance with a *chōnan*, an eldest son, who is saddled with parents. He has never mentioned the existence of healthy grandparents.

Aunt Shizu, who held one of the largest roles in the narratives of family life ten years ago, remains to be accounted for. Her career has become one of nobility, without title but with much acclaim. Returning to Takashima after 15 years of employment in Osaka as cook, housemother, and general factotum in a company residence for single men, she arrived financially armed with a small pension and the ownership of her house on Takashima and a little farm-land. Her self-sacrifice and endurance in seeing her nephew Jiro through college are admired by everyone. She regards her present conditions of life as much better than those she knew in Osaka, where, as she often says, the air was always worse than that of Takashima even at the height of its *kōgai*. Her income is modest, but enough for someone so versed in thrift as she. Now 69 and bothered a little by a high cholesterol level that led her doctor to forbid her to eat pork, which together with chicken have become staples in the Taka-shima diet, she is otherwise healthy. She has decided that she will live to age 85, alone. She misses the presence of the chickens she once raised, but raising chickens is now uneconomical and no family does so. Her nonhuman com-panions are a cat and a dog, both acquired as sickly strays that she nursed to health.

Shizu cultivates a kitchen garden, watches television, talks with local friends and relatives, and, often, travels by bus to nearby shrines and temples in the company of agemates, mostly female. Widowed and lacking children, she has no moral responsibility toward kin that involves money and no one feels more than casual responsibility toward her except her nephew Jiro. He and his wife have often invited Shizu to live with them, and she has stead-fastly declined. Reciprocity for her services in behalf of Jiro has already come to her by means of the respect accorded to her by the community, and this has given her much pleasure. A compatible combination of thrift and altruism have become ingrained in her, and these traits now constitute her career.

Since her return to Takashima, Shizu has followed a pattern of life established in Osaka. Selling a piece of her farmland for a high but altogether reasonable price to a neighboring family wishing to build a house for a second son, she turned the money over to her brother Hajime to allow the construction of the new dwelling for his and her parents. Selling another piece of land several years later at a much greater price to the shipbuilding company and adding to this sum the accumulation of some years of savings from her regular income, she aided niece Yuriko and her husband in buying an expensive house in central Kurashiki. This philanthropy left no clear possibility for future benevolence. Like others in the community, she directs her thoughts of financial altruism toward kin, and all of her relatives are provided for.

For Aunt Shizu, thrift has gradually become a goal rather than a means. She buys no costly foods, eats the vegetables and fruit that she herself raises, and practices similar thrift in all other things. She can easily afford gas or electric heating appliances, but she owns none, and, of course, the charcoal heaters of the past are impractical today because of problems of securing charcoal and the inconvenience of lighting it without the aid of a woodburning stove or firepit. On the coldest days of winter, when the temperature in her house becomes bone chilling, she retires to bed with her docile black cat, which, as she explains to anyone who is interested, has a body temperature higher than that of human beings and is therefore a good and safe heater. By these means, she is able to save a full half of her modest income. Her problem is to find a suitable use for that income.

Recommended Reading

Beardsley, Richard K., John W. Hall, and Robert E. Ward, 1959, *Village Japan*. Chicago: University of Chicago Press.

>A fine and extremely detailed study of a small farming community in central Japan. As with other community studies in this listing, a considerable part of its contents is now outdated.

Befu, Harumi, 1971, *Japan: An Anthropological Introduction*. San Francisco: Chandler Publishing Company.

>A short, comprehensive account of Japanese culture and society that includes a summary of prehistoric developments.

Benedict, Ruth, 1946, *The Chrysanthemum and the Sword*. Cambridge, Mass.: The Riverside Press.

>An interesting and perceptive study of ideal Japanese values. Outdated at the time of its publication, the study is nevertheless valuable today.

Cornell, John B., and Robert J. Smith, 1956, *Two Japanese Villages*. Ann Arbor, Mich.: University of Michigan Press, Center for Japanese Studies, Occasional Papers No. 5.

>Studies of a mountain community and a farming community of central Japan based upon field research conducted in the early 1950s.

Dore, R. P., 1973, *British Factory–Japanese Factory*. London: George Allen & Unwin Ltd.

>A detailed comparison of a Japanese and a British factory that relates their similarities and differences to the cultural traditions of the two societies.

De Vos, George A., with contributions by Hiroshi Wagatsuma, William Caudill, and Keiichi Mizushima, 1973, *Socialization for Achievement, Essays on the Cultural Psychology of the Japanese*. Berkeley: University of California Press.

>A large collection of interpretive writings centered on the ways on which values and goals, such as motivation toward achievement, are inculcated and reinforced among the Japanese.

Doi, Takeo, 1973, *The Anatomy of Dependence*, trans, by John Bester. Tokyo: Kodansha.

>An engrossing psychological interpretation of interpersonal relations and emotional dependency among the Japanese.

Embree, John F., 1939, *Suye Mura, A Japanese Village*. Chicago: University of Chicago Press.

The "classic" community study of Japan, an account of a community of Kyushu based upon field research conducted in 1936.

Fukutake, Tadashi, 1974, *Japanese Society Today*. Tokyo: University of Tokyo Press.

An informative, factual account that presents data covering the range of major sociological topics of study.

Hern, Lafcadio, *Japan: An Attempt at Interpretation*. Tokyo and Rutland, Vt.: Charles E. Tuttle Co., 1955 (first published, 1904).

An old but still useful, and highly readable, account of themes and values in Japanese culture.

Nakane, Chie, 1970, *Japanese Society*. Berkeley: University of California Press.

An interpretation of Japanese society by a Japanese anthropologist that emphasizes the subject of group identity in its relationship to individuality.

Norbeck, Edward, 1970, *Religion and Society in Modern Japan*. Houston: Tourmaline Press. (also *Rice University Studies*, Vol. 56, No. 1.)

A descriptive and interpretive study of Japanese religions, old and new, relating them to other social factors.

Norbeck, Edward, and Susan Parman, eds., 1970, *The Study of Japan in the Behavioral Sciences. Rice University Studies*, Vol. 56, No. 4.

A collection of writings by anthropologists, sociologists, and social psychologists summarizing research on Japan in their fields.

Reischauer, E. O., 1964, *Japan, Past and Present*, 3d ed., rev. New York: Alfred A. Knopf, Inc.

A fine short account of Japanese history by a distinguished scholar and former American ambassador to Japan.

Smith, R. J., and R. K. Beardsley, eds., 1962, *Japanese Culture, Its Development and Characteristics*. Viking Fund Publications in Anthropology, No. 34, and Chicago: Aldine Publishing Company.

Contains many useful articles by Japanese and American scholars concerning Japanese culture, society, and personality.

Von Mehren, Arthur Taylor, ed., 1963, *Law in Japan; The Legal Order in a Changing Society*. Cambridge, Mass.: Harvard University Press.

A fine book prepared by sociologically sophisticated Japanese scholars of law.

Vogel, Ezra F., 1963, *Japan's New Middle Class*. Berkeley: University of California Press.

Based principally upon the detailed study, conducted in 1958–1960, of six families living in a suburb of Tokyo. Now partly outdated but still informative.